Management Uncovered: Trends and Insights from India

PREFACE

Hey there, "wave"! How's it going? I'm your friendly neighborhood book editor, here to tell you about this amazing book that just landed on our shelves. It's a gem that our awesome publishing company has brought to life. Now, as part of my job, I get to dive into countless books, and I must say, this one is an absolute delight. No need for any unnecessary delay, let me give you a sneak peek into what makes it so worthwhile. Are you ready? Let's jump right in with the introductionManagement education is often perceived as elitist, as it tends to attract young men and women who are primarily driven by the perceived benefits associated with it. In India, higher education, especially in the field of management, has experienced significant growth, with numerous institutes offering management programs commonly referred to as Business Schools. This study examines the prevailing trends in management education in India and seeks to uncover its impact on both the industry and individuals. Furthermore, it delves into the emerging issues within the realm of management education and explores potential directions and policies for enhancing management education in India.The roots of management education can be traced back to the 18th century. Over the centuries, it has undergone substantial changes and developments, primarily drawing inspiration from Western management theories and practices. Occasionally, management institutions incorporate insights from Indian epics, scriptures, and traditions. It's noteworthy that management as a discipline has evolved from fundamental fields such as philosophy, psychology, economics, accounting, computer science, mathematics, statistics, and industrial engineering

In India, management education is often seen as catering to an elite audience. Frequently, young individuals are drawn to management education not solely for the purpose of gaining knowledge, exposure, and experience to contribute positively to society, but rather due to the allure of the perceived benefits associated with it.

To Dad, Mom, and my supportive colleagues, Your love, guidance, and unwavering support have been the driving force behind my journey as a writer. Thank you for believing in me and encouraging me to pursue my dreams. Your presence in my life has made all the difference.

With heartfelt gratitude,

ELIO.E

Copyright © 2022 By Elio Endless.
All rights reserved. No part of this book may be used or reproduced in any form whatsoever without written permission except in the case of brief quotations in critical articles or reviews. Printed in the United States of America.

For more information or to book an event, please contact: global.publishers@elioendless.com
Website: https://elioendless.com

Book design by Kai
Cover design by Tyson

Paperback ISBN:
ebook ISBN:

ElioEndless

ACKNOWLEDGMENTS

I would like to take this opportunity to extend my heartfelt thanks to all the individuals who have played a significant role in the creation of this non-fiction book. Your unwavering support, valuable advice, and constant encouragement have been invaluable throughout this journey. I am deeply grateful to those who have provided me with aspirational direction, constructive criticism, and kind advice. Your feedback has been instrumental in shaping the content and direction of this book. I genuinely appreciate your candid insights into my project. I am particularly grateful for the exceptional assistance of Mr. Jaffer and Mrs. Sameena at Endless Publishers. Their continuous support, dedication, and guidance have been instrumental in helping me overcome obstacles and improve the quality of my work. I am sincerely appreciative of their tremendous efforts and unwavering belief in this project. I would also like to express my heartfelt appreciation to Mr. Ahmed, my project's external advisor from Ahmed Corporation. His invaluable advice, insightful critique, and vast wisdom have played a pivotal role in refining my thoughts and enhancing the overall quality of this book. I am truly grateful for his guidance and expertise. Furthermore, I would like to acknowledge Ms. Sultana and every individual who has contributed to obtaining the necessary resources and making this initiative possible. Your assistance, whether it was in sourcing information, conducting research, or providing logistical support, is deeply appreciated. This book would not have come to fruition without your invaluable contributions. I cannot overlook the individual who initially sparked the flame of inspiration within me to embark on this book-writing endeavor.

Your unwavering belief in my abilities, continuous motivation, and unending support throughout this artistic process have been instrumental in my journey. I am forever indebted to you for being my constant source of inspiration. I want to express my deepest gratitude to every person who has contributed to this project, no matter how small their role may have been. Each and every one of you has played a part in making this book possible, and your contributions have not gone unnoticed. Your support, encouragement, and assistance have been instrumental in bringing this book to fruition. Finally, I would like to give special credit to Kai, B.EE, and Tyson, the pen names that have accompanied me on this writing adventure. Your creativity, distinct perspectives, and unique insights have added depth and character to this book. I am honored to have had the opportunity to collaborate with you. To all of you who have been a part of this remarkable journey, I extend my deepest gratitude. Your unwavering support, guidance, and friendship have been invaluable. Thank you for believing in me and for contributing to the realization of this non-fiction book. With

sincere appreciation,
Elio Endless

EDITOR NOTE

1. Publisher Notes: This edition is a product of inspiration from other works, with a portion of its content derived from public domain sources. Elioendless, the creator, editor, and publisher of the ebook edition, utilized manuscripts, select texts, and illustrative images from public domain archives. Members can acquire this ebook from our website for personal use. However, please note that any form of commercial storage, transmission, or reverse engineering of this file is strictly prohibited.

Table of Contents

Preface..
Dedication..
Copyright ....
Acknowledgement...............................
Chapter One ....
Chapter Two...
Chapter Three ....
Chapter Four ....
Chapter Five ....
Chapter Six ....

CHAPTER 1
INTRODUCTION

CHAPTER 1
INTRODUCTION
Enhancing Industry Collaboration in Business Education

The scholastic educational programs contains an a lot of Skill increase course like Communication, headship, database Modeling, consumer Orientation, advance and Design thoughts and Sustainability.

The world's second-most packed nation, India is the world's main dealer of administration instruction. In any case, that scale gives a false representation of issues. Various business colleges offer substandard instruction, has beforehand researched, and littler foundations battle to remain above water. A fourth of business colleges in India take in less than 60 hopefuls in every yearly mate, a class measure that AIMA, the All-India Management Association, a national affiliation bearing industry body, calls "wretchedly low".

Regardless of whether in an especially went to balanced or not, the work prospects for Indian business understudies have in like way dropped, as showed up by AIMA. The expense of courses has widened—even in the most unimportant quality schools—while the remuneration graduates can should need to get is falling. "There various individuals continuing ahead from business colleges who don't land positions in metro urban systems or gigantic affiliations," says Rajan Saxena, the opposite standard of direct chancellor of the Narsee Monjee Institute of Management Studies, an enlightening cost based school in Mumbai, and executive of the standard mix of totals at AIMA. This is customarily down to solid test for all around couple of positions, yet in like way a refinement among lighting up and head necessities.

Such issues can hold down a nation that will require always grand quality specialists. So as 2015 changed into 2016, AIMA scattered a structure research, seven months really accomplishing fulfillment, from a board contributed with perceiving how to refresh alliance course in the nation. The objective is striking: "By 2025 [the] Indian affiliation heading structure ought to unmistakably rise as the accompanying best on earth, second just to that of [the] USA."

AIMA proposes tearing down areas that have propped up business heading in India for a basic long time. Composed informational modules have been standard, says Dr Saxena. Regardless, there is a titanic opening between India's best business colleges (Ahmedabad's Indian Institute of Management (IIM-A) tops The Economist's general organizing of business colleges' concerning opening new occupation openings) and its undeniably customary universities. In any case both of them show a near theory and procedures. That isn't right headed. A MBA continuing forward from a business college in Kapurthala (masses: 99,000) is out and out less in danger to achieve the fundamental body of an overall firm than one leaving an administration organization in Mumbai (populace: 12m). The aptitudes expected to deal with a littler organization—in Indian overwhelming industry, for instance—are diverse to worldwide enterprises.

Business enterprise would be more qualified to littler schools, Dr Saxena reasons, and would improve India. A few schools offer courses on bootstrapping organizations, yet it ought to wind up a center piece of the instruction framework. Coordination with industry would help target enlightening endeavors to suit the necessities of relationship, too. Bit is head: the social affair endorses interfacing supporters to the best 150 business universities to battle on a general market by improving staff and workplaces, and repositioning the remaining 4,600 or so schools better to serve relationship on a national or near estimation.

AIMA's case that India's business schools can approach those in America inside 10 years is certainly an abundance of attempting. Regardless, it should, in any occasion, be possible to move as an inside point for everything considered association heading. For the world's most discernible business school report, that is the scarcest that ought not out of the ordinary.

Ethical Dimensions in Teaching

Powerful instructing requires settling on troublesome and principled decisions, practicing cautious judgment, and respecting the unpredictable idea of the instructive mission. Notwithstanding the specialized information and aptitudes instructors need to use in their day by day hone, they should likewise know about the moral measurements of their calling. In this light, the essential mission is to cultivate the improvement of abilities, auras, and comprehension, while recognizing insightfully and capably an extensive variety of human needs and conditions. In this way, instructors must ace a collection of instructional techniques and systems, yet stay basic and intelligent concerning their training (National Board for Professional education principles, 1998).

Better mindfulness and press forward in perfection boast made various instructional methods accessible today with the instructors, for example, contextual investigation techniques, reenactments, PowerPoint introductions, pretend, assignments, blackboard educating and so on. An educator needs to settle on a balanced decision of at least one of these teaching methods. In any case, the utilization of the inventive techniques for educating learning requires preparing and mastery with respect to the educator. This modified goes for cultivating inventive showing abilities in the personnel of administration establishments. These abilities incorporate exercises, circumstance taking care of, ventures, motion pictures, recordings, internet based life and so forth. Furthermore, the customized goes for cleaning the educators' aptitude in the utilization of contextual analyses, recreations, pretend and so forth.

Developments in Teaching

- Activity and Project-based Teaching

- Audio-visual Advertisements

- Movie-based Teaching

- Situation Handling and Role Plays

- Video-based Case lets

- Teaching through Social Media

- Teaching through Videos/video cuts

- Teaching through Historical Cases and Narratives

IIMs have assumed a huge job in understanding the societal goals of India turning into an inventive, humane, and created country. This needs consideration everything being equal. Not very many individuals realize that IIMs contribute to such an extent, if not more, to open activity and administration with regards to the private part administration. The reason for this class is to proactively build request which will push IIMs to explicitly express their duties to the overall population and be set up for difficulties ahead. A segment of the key issues discussed in this Colloquium are:

☐ The shapes through which IIMs have portrayed their targets and orientation consistently.

☐ Adequacy of exercises taken by IIMs to make increasingly conspicuous social, good, and master duty among understudies and chairmen arranged at IIMs.

☐ IIMs' association building occupation and its impact on the idea of organization preparing and practice in India.

☐ Factors adding to the elitist character of IIMs and its social setting and centrality.

☐ The potential for IIMs expecting a reactant work in empowering, drawing in or serving the little scale, muddled/under-administered regions and other regular society affiliations.

☐ The work that IIMs witness for themselves in structure India into a made nation. The going with centers rose up out of the trade:

- IIMs have made a monstrous pledge to the Indian economy by giving corporate activity. The capacities made and honed in IIMs should be extended to various parts and establishments.

- IIMs shape the foundation of our nation's financial accomplishment by professionalizing administration for all segments of the economy and giving the innovative, specialized, and talented faculty for unrivaled riches age.

- IIMs offer a model for administration training with open and legitimacy based confirmations, great and important educational programs, grounds position, and a general inspiration to be pertinent to the social needs.

- The participative, decentralized, and straightforward administration framework can create IIMs the good example for brilliance looking for foundations.

- If worldwide notoriety for particular commitment and institutional magnificence must be supported, IIMs would need to arrange their ways to deal with tending to circumstances in globalization.

- To increase social authenticity and regard of different partners, IIMs need to find a way to bring understudies from less special social foundations.

- Higher administration instruction establishments, for example, IIMs ought to build up an intelligible and convincing mental image of how they would need to add to the novel, distorted India. Visioning contain to be participative plus must comprise each one of the associates.

IIM, Ahmedabad and London School of finances;

- There is a lot of proper blue distress and unease and also not cultivated payment about the condition of face line preparing in India. Many believe that the present agreement of front line prepare is elitist and ought not be shattered further. Then again, most educationists are concerned over the low idea of instructing and research in a colossal piece of our enlightening establishments. They underscore the essential for amazingly progressively indisputable assets at whatever point moved preparing is to value of the name and if in any event a few relationship of higher knowledge in India are to be first-rate and think about the very much many-sided needs of an information society. In the new cosmos of globalization, it is knowledge and research and aptitude which will present high ground to a land and not trashy uncouth vocation or even regular assets. Are we not living on the money made in the early broaden lengths of Independence by the image of a Nehru or a Bhabha or a Mahalanobis

To see in your mind eye so as to we can maintain a strategic distance from this total and wherever is tricky. In the interim, it can't be denied that these

alleged first class establishments do have some social duties. To increase social authenticity and regard of different partners, it winds up unavoidable for such

- institutions to find a way to mitigate the circumstance. Let me simply specify a couple of things which are sobbing for consideration.

- Basic ability is appropriated decently broadly and consistently in the general public. What one desires to defeat and destroy it to the best is furthest away point building. What ladder have particular or able establishments, for example, IITs and IIMs taken to attain such a goal?

- Given the shameful checks of section in the relations of cutting edge instruction, simply the most exemplary can achieve such foundations. This is not out of the ordinary. Be that as it may, actually, to increase social authenticity and regard of different partners, such establishments need to find a way to bring understudies from less favored social foundations. Indian managerial administration attempted and prevailing in this mission.

- When monetarily frail understudies do enter such tip top organizations, there is a want to give them monetary and other help to reject the weight on their family. A store of Rs 2.5 million be ready for such a reason quite a while prior at IIMA. We have to check the compelling use of the reserve till as of late and the proactive advances taken to connect with such understudies.

- There are a few reason why understudies from establishment like IIMs go to well-paying business occupations. A significant part of general society division does not have the hierarchical condition to ingest the abilities and points of view that such understudies are outfitted with. Be that as it may, one could endeavor to give motivating forces to understudies to urge them to go to communal and under-oversaw parts. For model, one force discount the credit or forfeit the advance of such understudies who exit to such subdivision although for a connect of years. Each formative organization needs to cross-sponsor. For what reason can't the happier understudies pay all the more with the goal that the less special understudies can save money and some go to work for NGOs or such different establishments at the masses in the open field? The pyramid for public climbing is persuade the chance to be ever more remarkable and understandably ludicrous with portion of time. The base from which elites are haggard and the throwing a ticket open which they serve is getting to be more slender. Will the pyramid end up compliment? Will IIMs find a way to bring youthful understudies and expert administrators from different social streams into their first class club with the goal that the world class themselves turn out to be all the more socially adjusted and responsive? All things considered, the independence these foundations have appreciated and great deservedly additionally cast on them more noteworthy social duty. There is no chance to get by which the interest for such a responsibility can be expelled as a superfluous approach their entryways.

IIM, Ahmadabad;, open issues focus, Bangalore

IIMs were built up by the direction of India as a piece of its industrialization and rejuvenation system. IITs had just arrived and supervision training was view as a reciprocal role alongside innovation for the renovation of the Indian cutback. It clarifies why these two preparations of organization were bring inside the domain of the particular teaching wing of the Ministry of teaching. The general population acknowledgment about most organization of higher education is that they are elitist. There is zilch astonishing on the subject of it as they make available food to a great extent to rather little and select gatherings of youngsters whose guardians could give them a decent training. Among such organizations, IIMs emerge due to the high hindrances to passage into these establishments, situation of their alumnae in the company division, and the universal open doors that get nearer their direction.

However, the foremost news about them in the medium for the most part relate to the tall pay rates offered to the fresh graduates nearly as however pay is an agent for perfection! Little else was poised about them in the press awaiting the shocking 'charge' issue went along. It only carrying weapons the elitist portrait of IIMs. However, the persons who traditional these organizations were forced by their potential for professionalizing supervision. They may have known on the elitist trap en route still that would not have not permitted them from taking the course they did. The primary three IIMs to be set up were absolutely watchful of the bigger job they wanted to play in the country's advancement.

At IIMB, present was a goal-oriented exertion to deal with the administration issues of an assortment of areas past industry. A decent arrangement of research, preparing, and counseling was hence improved the situation the administration, social areas, and other non-corporate parts. The reality remains, be that as it may, that these activities did not result in a critical broadening of the IIM modified.

The company area center reserved on being the prevailing and the nearly all obvious picture of all IIMs. It is stable to perceive any reason why this has continuous. Some may contend that IIMs did not an adequate amount of features their work ancient times the private corporate part. In spite of the fact that there is some reality in it, I question particularly that more forceful reputation would have made a difference. There were more imperative and inconspicuous components at work. As a matter of first importance, administration information and educational module have advanced around the shared division and it is this pool of culture, ideas, and devices with the intention of the IIMs obtained commencing abroad. It made it simpler for IIMs to dispose bespoke and attempt consultancy for the business segment. Regardless of whether IIMs put resources into research to create learning on different segments, it would have required some investment. In this way, there be a head begin factor for portion the private corporate area. Second, there be more noteworthy response to IIMs from the business division than from dissimilar parts and open organization. The post-graduate and bureaucrat customized be the best precedent. The corporate section ingested all the new-fangled alumnae. IIMB's alumnae who represented extensive authority in unlike areas did not discover apposite arrangement. These specializations be later on suspended. Counseling work was similarly besieged by the business. Government organization that seriously require administration abilities have numerous imperatives in enlisting IIM graduates and going to official customized. Their strategies and pay arrangements are to such an extent that they can't adequately contend with the confidential business segment. Underserved parts, for example, cooperative or wellbeing may income considerably more from present day administration yet they can't or not roused enough to react. Also, this is exacerbated even by the considerably higher pay rates and vocation prospects corporate can offer to the new alumnae. Third, there is a exceptional issue that is unworkable to miss to the admin.

The administrations staff may go to IIM modified yet are frequently out of shape to apply their new knowledge in their settings. Either the structure may not allow it or supporting new opinion ends up troublesome in an management that does not recompense them. This was the matter with IIMA-National Academy synchronized effort. The tailored got off to a decent begin when the IIMA labor force was specifically built-in. Be that as it may, when this moment of joint work was completed the Academy was not able continue the personalized with a similar energy. Figures, for example, changes authority and workforce may well have been in charge of this decay. Many counseling assignments for the administration may likewise have had a comparable destiny. Given this situation, it isn't astounding that IIMs have been commanded by their corporate area center. It won't be anything but difficult to turn around or debilitate this pattern. Yet, most likely, IIMs can find a way to address the necessities of different segments that are dangerous for the nation and the management. Indeed, even the confidential business college in the West have differentiate their work thusly. Driving business colleges in the US, for instance, have made unique projects for little business visionaries, the homestead part, and non-legislative associations. Some of them have supported research on the issues of these associations.

There are devoted staff bunches who distribute regarding these matters. There is no motivation behind why this is impossible in India by the freely financed IIMs. Nobody ought to be under the trick that this move will wipe out the elitist stomp on IIMs. The undertaking have to to be to make the wisest decision for the nation. As noted over, a few IIMs have just propelled activities that go past the private corporate area. An ongoing precedent is the configuration of the middle for Public Policy at IIMB so as to has a long haul modified for focal and state height authorities. Maybe, they are not adequately announce and consequently might not be completely recognized to the circles that issue. Obviously, significantly more should be complete past standing. What ladder should IIMs take to go toward this path?

- There are various approaches to urge workforce and sheets to suppose thusly. One that has been left for at IIMA is a workforce group on Future Directions so as to ponders and suggests a plan for activity. Another choice is to deliberately counsel with various partners (not just the corporate) who may have helpful plans to offer. This suggests, obviously, that the establishments and their administration including the personnel will introspect and search for innovative thoughts. It is the greatest way to keep away from others near enough their stimulus on IIMs. The activity for adjust should make from in.

- International skill unmistakably demonstrate that new activities continuously call for new venture and devoted gatherings. It is no matter which but difficult to create one study regarding a topic or to offer a course on a on one occasion foundation. Be that as it may, to create calculated information on a division or to grow new ideas and instrument, longer-term speculation and collaboration will be required. The sort of house work to be done to obtain this going won't occur without a reasonable proportion of inner agreement and institutional help.

- Institutional self-governance and adaptability are pre-requirements for doing the diverse things specified previously. It is improbable that the individuals who look to the administration to be told what they ought to do will influence utilization of the self-governance they to have. Numerous instructive organizations are kept running in a bureaucratic style. Self-sufficiency is by all accounts squandered on them. The conventions of IIMs in their first years were in total different from this style. It was normal for them to impact the administration thoughts and opinion for IIMs. I trust that the additional up to date IIMs will gain as of this experience and meeting and watch and exploit their self-rule to the finest of their capacity

Pradip N Khandwalla Former Director, IIM, Ahmedabad

Educator Anil Gupta has represented an extreme arrangement of inquiries concerning the problems of IIMs with regards to the faceoff among IIMs and its main funder, the legislature. The crisis appears to have left because of political reason. Be that as it may, it could repeat, in the same or different structures, inasmuch as the reliance on the administration isn't tended to. I am no place close as acquainted with alternate IIMs as I am with IIMA, everywhere I put in with reference to 27 years of my experienced life. Along these lines, my comments relate essentially to IIMA, however I trust they are not entirely insignificant to alternate IIMs. The pressure between a main funder and a foundation of scholastic magnificence is a proceeding with one however on the off chance that IIMA holds its real qualities and reacts inventively and viably to these strains, it will rise more grounded. Let me first rundown the qualities that IIMA, and by and large all foundations of xcellence, must hold or create. Above all else, IIMA emerges as one of only a handful couple of establishments in India with the purpose of has a justly participative, decentralized, and simple administration structure.

In principle, each one of the forces are vested in the Board of senate and the administrator. In all actuality, a significant part of the basic leadership is with the boards of trustees and people. The personnel, for example, through different panels, has significant say in the determination of the understudies and employees, in workforce advancements, in the substance of the scholarly and preparing programs that are offered, in the examination that is subsidized, and even such budgetary choices as the settling of the expenses. Singular employees have opportunity to outline new courses and preparing programs, settle on the route substance and education method, and what investigate to attempt. Not that the fundamental management process is a even one. It is frequently fierce and at era irritatingly moderate.

In any case, the procedure about mirrors the sort of popularity based and participative common society that we struggle for. In this intelligence, IIMA is a good example for all the perfection looking for establishments of this nation. They all have a stake in the greatness through-self-rule of IIMA. Their help merits developing in the present emergency. Besides, nobody so far has soundly indicated any hanky-panky in IIMA's option of understudies and employees. Here once additional, IIMA is a high-quality example for some establishments as far as institutional uprightness. The last is a rare item. No legislature in its correct personality would need to place it in hazard through its activities. The third excellence of IIMA is its institutional innovativeness. It has not just brought forth a few scholastic and preparing projects of generally perceived perfection, these projects themselves are persistently being re-developed. In numerous scholastic organizations of India, the syllabi barely alter in 10 years and course are pretty much solidified in time while the important fields of in order go running.

At IIMA, basically every course experiences some change or the other consistently — as far as readings, tests, extends or even teaching method. In some random year, at least twelve new courses and preparing projects might be on offer. There is a gigantic reinforcement for what is educated in the classroom as several Indian contextual investigations, explore discoveries, and instructing takes note of that feature the Indian, and progressively, the worldwide setting. I don't have the most recent figures. In any case, my gauge is that, all through the years,

. Throughout the decades, it shaped focuses and gatherings to add to the compelling administration of farming and country improvement, formative organization, populace control, vitality, wellbeing, and instruction. These gatherings have broadened the effect of IIMA well what went before the corporate area.

This commitment of IIMA additionally isn't sufficiently known. Once more, no significant partner in IIMA would need to melt this limit of IIMA to add, through research, prepare, and counseling, and reinstate what are recognized as the need segment of our universal public. There are many more commitment of IIMA. Be that as it may, I will specify just a single more. On the off chance that expert administration has turned into a regarded expression in India, a nation in which business, in the relatively recent past, was viewed as a corrupt movement; critical credit should most likely go to IIMs, astonishingly to IIMA. On account of IITs and IIMs, the homeland is situated high among the budding financial system on the nature of its particular and secretarial labor. This ability pool is an intense factor in pull in expanding distant speculation to India and in the globalization of Indian manufacturing. It would cost the state dear to weaken this promise.

Obviously IIMA has its wart. It has be reasonable in getting a grip on the open doors opened up by globalization. The better part of the graduates of its Post-Graduate plan (PGP) have a leaning to settle on easy occupations in easy organization for cushy compensate and livens as opposed to demonstrate their backbone as business people or as ambitious innovators in powerful organizations short on proficient administration. IIMA could complete much more to cultivate in its understudies a more grounded feeling of business morals and business social compulsion, two region in which IIMA strength fall behind its companion in the West. It is up till now to build up an intelligible and convincing vision of what it needs to add to the new, changed, yet at the same time exceptionally poor India.

It could have contribute all the more vehemently and viably to such require divisions as the squeaky Indian management structure that has be such a holdup our individual satisfaction. There is a fear that the IIMA be stuck on a level. It needs to re-charge its batteries. forceful visioning is a process that can allow organization to like IIMA to jump from one level of operational to in total larger amounts of magnitude. I advocate four components of total visioning by IIMA

• The principal module is one of institutional degree. What genus of a profile, from beginning to end increase and broadening, acquisition and divestments, multiparty endeavors, internationalization of exercises, and so forth., does IIMA require to contain, say, by 2010?

• The second section includes the visioning of institutional effecting by 2010 as far as global rankings, instructive and investigates quality, and income to anchor money related independence.

• The third component includes the visioning of the nature of working by 2010, say, as far as the professionalization of decision-making employees plus far superior association, speedier and more expertisebased participative essential management, and more noteworthy business enterprise in recognizing and getting a handle on the open doors managed by financial development and globalization.

- The fourth element is the thing that IIMA be supposed to add to the admin scene and to the individual approval in India.

Before, IIMA has, obviously, occupied with visioning works out, principally through the gadget of the Committee on Future Directions set up like clockwork or somewhere in the vicinity. Its considerations have included most partners and its report is generally talked about inside. A portion of its proposals are executed. Be that as it may, in my experience, the execution has been for the most part very late thus the effect and the advantages have been constrained

Visioning must be participative and must include every one of the partners. With regards to IIMs, it must include the staff and the Board, as well as the graduated class, the understudies, the different parts served by the base, and in addition the legislature. Since the process of visioning is as very important as the dream itself, the help of at least one process advisors might be helpful in guarantee that the procedure is participative, there is enough conceptualizing for creative viewpoints plus choices, and likewise, there is a powerful technique for achieving an agreement on the institutional dream. Retreats help thus might Devil's backing to pledge that the vision has foresee the preponderance of the conceivable obstacles.

Visioning is an doings in pie in the sky taking into account if there is no possible usage system. Visioning have to be joined by a usage method that breaks the responsibility of settled upon alter into missions, exacting assignments, structure of implementation with particular accountabilities plus courses of events, observing and audit systems and timetables, motivating forces for brilliance in execution, et cetera. Circumstances are different. There is much more rivalry now; openings are currently coming thick and quick, however vanish rapidly, as well, if not got a handle on in time. Vision, innovativeness, endeavor, and powerful usage are the paddles with which IIMA must row into vaster waters.

Amitava Bose past boss and Presently university lecturer, IIM, Calcutta

The vision by means of which IIMs be set up be a dream with a modification. Unquestionably, it was by no means the object that IIMs would be copy of customary business school that think the supplies of the private business part metaphorically speaking. They were envision as association relations that would be prepared for offering a clarification to an impressively increasingly broad societal request. The idea was to make chairmen who may play out no perspiration paying little mind to where they might be found. Regardless, close to the day's end, the request remnants: how much shock has this complete.

The most observable of all IIM behavior is the PGP. Most faultfinders of IIMs battle that the penalty of the PGP have just benefitted the confidential corporate separation and remote multinational. That couldn't have be the objective with which the administration of India set up these establishment and finance them. Intellectuals should need to see a more prominent measure of our understudies keeping an eye on top of the necessities of open foundations including open utilities. They would be more and more happy if our understudies had better the manner in which our railways are sprint, the route expansion in our urban network is controlled, and the means by which our restoration focuses are administer. They make known that our understudies encompass not kept an eye on the necessities of the affirmed 'undermanaged' sections of our country

There is a sense anywhere the PGP is boldly 'elitist.' It is an incredibly particular program. It can't yet be specific since it is legitimize driven. The people who don't have the cut-off authenticity can't get in. There is one more point that is critical here. Organization guidance is exhibit driven such that school preparing when all is said in done isn't. Because of the high legitimacy increased in value by the meritocratic PGP, astonishing positions are ensured for its things. This has started progressively of the most splendid understudies of the land to take a stab at affirmations here. In this way, IIM understudies are among the best in the country .The best understudies will require the best occupations. This is reality. Regardless, the best vocations are nowadays described similar to cash and power. As gatekeepers, we shove our brood always toward employments promising ensured cash and power. It may be awful yet it can't be deprived of that the best vocation are not in the 'under-regulated' portions but in its place in the confidential corporate separation and with multinational. In viewpoint on the group of the advantage point of view, these occupations are moreover by and large mentioning. Meanwhile, rewards for prominent execution are quick in striking separation to 'progression by-rank when-an opening rises' in government and general society part. If the 'under-managed' division need to agreement from IIMs, they be supposed to improve their absorptive point of confinement.

An a legitimate model is just the IIMs. Could IIMs enroll their very own understudies as boss? Do IIMs certification engaging regulatory callings? The more prepared IIMs explicitly are straddled with managerial rigidities which are out of row with the challenge of the modern world.

IIMs are not supreme. They may enterprise yet are likely not going to change politically tricky HR system in the party portion. Yet again, they may venture anyhow are most likely not going to change tendencies of the forefront parent or desires of the present youth. There is, thusly, only a solitary course by which IIMs can get their things to go to the 'under-directed' zones: they comprise to move themselves so as to go away from the rationally most predictable understudies. One manner to deal with do with the purpose of is account that IIMs are not leaving to offer place benefits and to alter the instructive project to refute 'Westernized' subjects, for instance, present day cash related organization, essential organization, etc., and present greater estimations of open service oriented course. What is firm, regardless, is that a mixture of employees would not agree to such a adjust. In like behavior, which adjust would need to witness the IIM imprint worth getting scattered? Thusly, that is the spot the issue lies. Clearly, when the best understudies quit pending in, the best staff would in like way pack up and go. There are various hard to believe private establishment which will use the flight.

So to speak, given the option of the earth, IIMs are 'elitist' in the feeling of educational particularity. Tip top occupations and academic authenticity go as one. This may radiate an impression of being a tragic catch for growth. Notwithstanding, is it astonishingly a catch? There are a variety of who may fight that most development issues are non-academic in natural world and don't need insightful glory for their answer. Why not leave instructive brightness for schools to deal with? Transparently financed organization foundations should offer need to progress and if that infers discarding over the top diversion with academic accreditations by then so be it. The response to the above is the going with: While gaining ground toward insightful brightness does not therefore address the issues that should be tended to of progression, nonappearance of educational radiance does not normally urge promise to national improvement either. There are various schools starting at now in nearness which don't oblige the most splendid understudies. For what reason are the aftereffects of these schools not dealing with the crushing issues of progress organization? Is the organization effectively ingest them in the 'under-regulated' wreckage It would not be apt to attack the PGP of IIMs solely with respect to coordinate game plans. The PGP has set measures for a few distinct schools to imitate. The PGP prospectus has be used as a standard for different schools. Thus, IIMs have chemically influenced organization preparing in the country. Be that as it may, there is chance to show signs of development and I be supposed to need to create a physically powerful proposal. There is a firm proportion of duty that IIM staff gathering have be making to come within reach of making with respect to investigation, consultancy, and getting ready. My proposition needs to do with how to revamp a characteristic PGP understudy's thought with developmental issues of the state. The proposal is that the basics be supposed to take up marvelous on-going examination adventures thinking about assorted portions of the nation state and 'execute' these throughout the PGP. The word region is being used in a approximately plan and a small openly. These might be described in dissimilar ways. They could be portray similar to belongings (e.g., agro-based activities, for example, tea, sugar, etc.), organization (transport, manage, etc.), association (laid-back, modern offices, specialist rising, etc.), geography (ordinary Bengal, etc.) plus whatnot. The undertakings be supposed to be so illustrate as to require enormous field labor and the understudies be supposed to be alloted to put energy in the field as a section of the standard subjects. The steady work isn't the way by which to plan such endeavors yet to mastermind their execution. We would need the organization's help.The thought is by all accounts talented. In this way, not wholly would IIM understudies and educator add to the development writing (and accordingly to agreement making), the simple process of taking an interest in the field overviews would enhance their comprehension of the ground substances. The impact of this on new personalities can be relied upon to be extensive and perpetual.

K R S Murthy Former Director, IIM, Bangalore

The social location of exclusiveness in association preparing has distorted basically since the fundamental two IIMs be set up throughout the 1960s. Exactly at what time India set out on mastermind fiscal improvement, the need was felt for creators and boss. Industry was new to the bleeding edge organization thoughts, techniques and methodology. IIMs were to exhibit current organization guidance in India. Its alumni were to improve the supply of originators from IITs. Orchestrating was done to alter the supply of establishment and chiefs with the emblematic desires of the production. Nevertheless, this modify did not transpire at the minute scale rank in light of the verity that the fantastic and overpowering organization were basically controlled by the association, while the graduate class of both IITs and IIMs preferential a variety of streets. The test for IIMs was to study and get used to the American group preparing and rehearses, alter them to the Indian scenery through research, get a feel for Indian industry with present day society techniques and strategy, and find game plan open entryways for the graduates. In the early years, the IIMA Board work calmly like a self-supervising civilization. There was strong help from the state and central government. The fluid commencement situation, the tall activity, and the idea of direction pioneers in the legislative body engaged the institute of key discontinuities in province, in the choice of cohort, in relations with the state government, the combine and Ford Foundation, as correspondingly in enlisting the combined effort and backing of manufacturing. The Board of Governors intervene and urged institutional association to enlist the requisite assistance from business and to give a good old fashioned thumping to authoritative rules and methodologies. In the meantime, IIMA furthermore set up staff social events to tackle agribusiness, dealing with a evidence, and a variety of parts. All jointly not to drive some additional load on the association expenditure plan, additional than so as to required intended for the PGP, the sectoral labor force packs be required to act usually finance, which in like manner busy them to be receptive and pertinent to pros. Private manufacturing saw the significant blame that the official designer and the alumni indoctrination specialist could create to regulatory do. The institute reputation and sureness extended. The division packs could give gigantic assistance to technique makers. Subsequently, though unfit to attract alumnae into its movements, the administration of India had productively enthused some basic and commercial elitist higher informational establishment. For a anthology of reasons, the revenue of alumni in commerce was high. In spite of the way that their authenticity, preparing, and potential were perceived, there were responses that the alumni were grandiose, driven, and extremist. I don't accept that they were any more so than some other social affair of productive energetic specialists. The employments that they finally chose were as contrasting as that of some other master gathering. Not once in a while finishes one keep running over IIM graduates who have pushed toward getting to be representatives, senior chairmen in non-government affiliations, open undertakings, and even joined basic organizations after centered examinations. Consequently, IIM graduates have contributed generally in different parts and domains.

During the 1960s, the social setting gave couple of alternatives as opposed to unbelievable and defended adolescents other than the IAS. In so as to particular condition, the clear and genuineness based route of action of IIMs give a decent not obligatory vocation choice. A consistently expanding number of young people competed for a probability, which was open free of rank, district, religion, or focus of pull together at the graduates level. The exclusivity started from realism and feat in contention. That is the way someplace the understudies get tune to beforehand, in the midst of, and past their instructive era in IIMs, a huge various trademark inverse the exclusiveness of the IAS units. For, the IIM alumnae despise forcing plan of action or administrative power that the IAS system get adjusted with. The bargain of IIM graduate class is excellent in correlation to the pact of the IAS. A festivity of the IIM graduate class is generally an individual and eager endeavor, with no of the components of authority of agreement of an IAS bunch. The open entryways that IIM alumnae get are easy to get to to non-elitists — non-IIM alumnae plus even no alumni — not in the slightest degree like the IAS. Their affiliations also need to fight, not in the least like the governing body.

The elitism of IIMs was in like manner in view of the fragment staff social affairs, which earned the liberality of course of action makers and master bodies, supporting their investigation inspects. The watchwords be social significance and distinction. During the

1970s, a gathering trainer of method and different leveled theory from Case Western preserve University to IIMA took a gander at the theory test yield of IIMA effort force with persons of his institution of higher education. His judgment was so as to while the subjects chosen by the labor force of his University be speculative and base scarcely on various level issues, the topic that the IIMA faculty chosen appeared, it seems that, to be fundamentally more and more broad in additional room and custody an eye on down to trade issues. For sure, even to the loss of not finding a stain in universal journals, the staff favored focus on work that be proper. Yet, a variety of private relations and school workplaces took after the instance of IIMs and started organization preparing programs, their number was not as much as a hundred. The IIMs stood isolated the extent that their work force, grounds, and various resources The elitist status of the associations and their alumni, ordinarily, offered rise to the request: for what reason should the council support the preparation of elitist overseers who serve private industry, especially the multinationals? The Government of India could have made the IIMs self-financing, with increasingly significant self-administration in settling the cost, and raising various resources. Be that as it may, it didn't. IIMs continued modifying their monetary plans and the various demands on them through a blend of undertaking sponsoring and government endowments.

The social setting changed during the 1970s, with the lawmaking body moving further towards all the more firmly government control of the economy. With nationalization of dealing with a record, coal, and various divisions, and the accentuation on dejection removal and natural headway, it was felt that there was a necessity for young alumni in individuals when all is said in done fragment. It was in such a social setting, and as a departure from the earlier IIMs, that IIMB was set up during the 1970s. Developing the experience of IIMA and IIMC, IIMB started on the as sumption that a model of organization, relevant to the immense and creating Indian open fragment, could be indigenously gathered and passed on. It didn't collaborate with any outside association. It expected that the lawmaking body and the overall public section would reinforce and ingest the yield. Again, that did not happen, though some open undertakings, with extraordinary activity, could pull in a segment of the IIM and non-IIM organization graduates to their affiliations. The IIM appear for organization guidance — its open and authenticity built certifications in light of an all-India reason, incredible and significant instructive projects, and grounds circumstance attempts, and a general motivation to be noteworthy to the social needs — was duplicated to different degrees by various non-public schools and even school organization divisions. The working of IIMs with various cognizant social occasions, level and participative essential initiative structures was an amazing departure from the working of a common school, with its hierarchic, non-responsive, and very politicized systems. While a couple of schools endeavored to give increasingly noticeable self-principle to their organization workplaces, the IIM model couldn't run in doubt be rehashed in the Universities and the schools as they couldn't set up the basic staff and various resources.

There has been a speedy improvement in organization preparing, beginning with the late 1980s and mid 1990s. There are at present right around 1,000 associations, which are advancing experts level preparing in organization, with a capacity to graduate more than 60,000 every year. The amount of establishments offering organization guidance in various application regions, for instance, prosperity has moreover extended. Elitist packs are extending in different zones — R&D, Information Technology, Biotechnology, Drugs and Pharmaceuticals, and the Capital Markets, with or without formal organization abilities.

The advancement main impetus has begun from the money related changes of the 1990s which has released private essentialness and movement. Likewise as the Indian helpers of the multinationals were the first to see the estimation of the IIM graduates during the 1960s, the new multinationals entering India have been expedient not solely to see the estimation of the graduated class of IIMs, yet what's more in seeing the potential for inspect composed exertion with Indian research foundations. Indian industry, under genuine worldwide contention, is getting the opportunity to be dynamic on Indian grounds just as on grounds abroad. Globalization has taken off. The media is tuned to the overall systems. It terms the IIMs as B-schools, slighting the consider choice organization, instead of business, in their amazingly names and the various ventures and activities that IIMs are locked in with. In this social setting, there is a need to reexamine the standards for greatness and congruity of India's elitist informational associations. IIMs require more efforts to make it effective.

In the mid-1990s, when the Government of India confronted a monetary crunch, it needed IIMs and IITs to wind up self-financing. IIMs could react better to this circumstance than IITs as they were self-governing. IITs, administered by the IIT Act, were more reliant on government endorsement for charge increments. A portion of the IITs needed to concede even genuinely necessary upkeep uses for quite a long while until the point that the legislature could favor charge update.

All the more as of late, the administration endeavored to force a scratch in the income stimulating by IIMs. Such coercive greatness of the governing body can hurt party building. In the arrangement of IIMs, the management has an tempting job. It select the Chairman, the plank persons, and the Director. In the continuing crisis regarding the accuse cut, Shri Narayana Murthy endeavored to interfere between the basics and the legislature. The dissatisfaction of the organization to take a additional goal and methodical viewpoint of the structure is infuriating.

In the rising universal social location, the management and power of tip top establishments must be exhaustive, adaptable, understanding. The Board ought to be free and self-governing. In my outlook, the Board ought to farm out the Chairman of the Board with the Director as on report of Indian foundation of Science, Bangalore. The Board would then be gifted to assume full danger for supervision. The Board can establish an arrangement of responsibility to every one of its partners. In foundations that canister be monetarily gratis, the Government's manage job can be restricted to investment in Board discourses plus supporting institutional exercises where conceivable. The administration capacity to arbitrate or set main beliefs ought to be incomplete to brief era of gross failing. The government and the state won't be a breakdown with such a alter. IIMs will scale more famous statures plus convey additional compensation to each one of its partners

CHAPTER 2
Future Directions and Recommendations

CHAPTER 2
Future Directions and Recommendations

Worldwide administration instruction has seen different difficulties in the ongoing past. Different researchers (Pfeffer and Fong, 2002 Leavitt, 1989 , Pfeffer and Fong, 2004 Ghoshal, 2005 O Toole, 2005) have featured unique, frequently clashing, explanations behind postgraduate administration training in the US getting to be rudderless. A hidden thought, rising up out of these researchers is that, weights from different sources like media, partners like understudies, have constrained administration foundations to receive hones that may bode well in the short run however are probably going to have genuine negative impacts over the long haul.

Quality has been characterized in business as conformance to determinations (Srabec, 2000). Garvin (1984) has given properties of value in item/benefit models (TQM) in business they are execution, highlights, unwavering quality, conformance, sturdiness, usefulness and saw quality.

Add up to quality administration is a general connection insight that hold that quality is conventional change (Seymour, 1992) and actions quality through clients' implementation with the relatives they enclose encountered.

W. Edwards Deming's chain response hypothesis, exhibits that better things are made by concentrating on such different zones as quantifiable examination of deformities, transport and association, client relations and representative correspondences. Subsequently, capability is stretched out as less things are rejected (Madu and Kuei, 1993)

Juran saw the expenses picked up by a relationship to keep up a specific element of critical worth. These are sorted out as: (1) Prevention costs, those costs used with a genuine target to keep non-obliging things or associations from happening and from achieving the buyer (2) Appraisal costs, those exhausted on keeping up quality measurements through estimation and examination of information to recognize and change issues (3) Internal disappointment costs, those that outcome from unsatisfactory quality that is found going before the vehicle of a thing or association to the client; and (4) External thwarted expectation costs, those that happen after low quality things or associations achieve the client. The motivation driving quality cost estimation and examination is to uncover the best association of a relationship to the bewildering cost of expelling quality issues (Madu and Kuei, 1993)

Quality is a precarious and inadequately described make (Parasuraman, Zeithaml and Berry, 1985). Quality is an unpredictable and badly arranged make to gauge in preferred position sections. The going with highlights portray the direction business, as an associations industry (Kotler, 2002) Services are immaterial getting ready can't be seen, achieved, heard or felt, before picking, it must be experienced.

Associations are vague there is speedy utilization of the association (direction) gave. Association quality moves the possibility of association differentiates every once in a while relying on the heads, kind of staff, foundation changes, library work environments gave, and so forth in conclusion preferences are momentary getting ready gave last semester/year can't be verified for use next semester/year.

Darker, Keonig and Harold (1993) recommend that solitary bearing to oversee evaluating quality is to utilize a sorted out strategy of solicitation. For instance, SERVQUAL records 10 general organization quality issues that are pondered from the point of view of the client (Parasuraman, Zeithaml, and Berry, 1985). In this way of thinking has been familiar with bleeding edge arranging (Davis and Allen, 1990) and the standard courses of action fortify examinations among schools (Brown, Keonig and Harold, 1993).

Mahapatra and Khan (2007) developed a scale called "EduQUAL" having 43 things drawn from SERVQUAL and different examinations. The scale was controlled to understudies, graduated class, watchmen of understudies and verification heads of various express establishments transversely over India. Factor examination demonstrated pressing alpha attributes for the going with estimations: learning results, responsiveness, physical work environments, character movement and scholastics.

Systematized referencing may have their targets. A couple of experts see that climb client concerns are the motivation behind mixing of fundamental worth and that quality is unpredictable to specific schools or classes of schools (Ewell, 1992; Keller, 1992).

Sahney, Banwet and Karunes (2006) composed a preliminary examination utilizing SERVQUAL estimations. The purpose of assembly of the examination was on perceiving a structure of system credits arranged to suit quality in direction and went for seeing and stirring up linkages and relationship between the client prerequisites (understudies of Engineering and Management) and the course of action attributes. The examination evaluated the affirmations and needs for understudies for both the client prerequisites and outline attributes. The holes among discernments and needs were considered. By utilizing interpretive assistant condition demonstrating a way examination containing free and ward components was made and tried utilizing quality utmost sending. QFD might be depicted as, 'a structure for spreading out a thing or an association in light of client requests and including all individuals from the alliance' (Maddux et al., 1991).

Sahney, Banwet and Karunes (2006) portrayed the way examination; nature of direction was the standard ward variable. The free factors were appropriate and productive association, clear and explicit systems and procedure, gear for assessment and control, especially depicted informative ventures graph, reasonableness and essentialness of educational modules content, enlightening tasks arranging, plan, rare audit, instructional wellbeing – wellness and sufficiency, instructional technique – class measure, sufficient, foundation and working environments are all around portrayed

Quality in teaching has been depict variedly as, magnificence in planning (Peters and Waterman, 198222), admiration development in way (Feigenbaum, 195123), agreement for cause (Reynolds, 198624; Brennan et al., 199225)

Prosperity of clearing up behind offered was prearranged by Tang and Zairi, (1998) in like way moreover health of instructive end result and occurrence for use Juran plus Gryna, (1988).

Gilmore (1974) depict quality in direction as conformance of receiving standing by regard organized objectives, points of importance and brass tacks (Gilmore, 1974; Crosby, 1979), frown shirking in preparation process (Crosby, 1979), and gathering or beating customers needs for receiving ready (Parasuraman et al., 1985).

Spanbauer depict TQM in in receipt of ready, as "TQM is an administration rationality which sets up frameworks and procedures to meet and surpass the desires for clients. It is a constant mission for nonstop change through documentation and the utilization of instruments in a critical thinking air that highlights group activity and great initiative practices (Spanbauer, 1995). TQM is referred to by various terms, for example, consistent process change (CPI), add up to quality administration (TQL) and persistent quality change (CQI). As indicated by Spanbauer, training is an administration with clients like some other business, and those clients express fulfillment and disappointment about school administrations and guidance.

Spanbauer (1995) recommends that the aftereffects of applying TQM in advanced education ought to be surveyed by four parameters: change in learning, change in institutional effectiveness, graduates having TQM skills and social change in the foundation.

Scrabec (2000) contends that in a TQM way to deal with quality in advanced education, the significant downside is thinking about the understudies as clients. The client driven methodology does not have an attention on who the essential clients are and who is to set the administration determinations. On the off chance that the TQM approach is taken after, an abnormal state of understudy fulfillment does not really quantify the nature of training; however it might be one marker.

Garvin (1984) has recognized TQM and TQE (Total Quality Education). Garvin has analyzed the properties of value in item/benefit models with quality instruction.

Scarbec (2000) opines that to operationalize the ideas of TQM to quality in instruction is extremely troublesome. Scrabec (2000) has proposed eight potential proportions of value instruction; they are institutionalized national tests, accreditation of instructive foundations, understudy fulfillment measures, industry criticism, universal content and quantitative measures, national lists, for example, licenses, legislature of free reviews to set models and understudy assessments.

Scrabec (2000) has given an aggregate quality instruction show in light of advantages and on quality training characteristics. The model shows beneficiary or understudy fulfillment because of an aggregate quality instruction approach, yet not the fundamental criticism to enhance the framework. This model enables understudy assessments to be a piece of the general procedure. The model uses inward reviewing to enhance the instruction procedure consistently.

Widrick, Mergen and Grant (2002) have estimated three quality measurements (nature of outline, nature of conformance and nature of execution) in advanced education. They have built up an arrangement of estimation parameters utilized in assessing the nature of research and educational modules advancement and the apparatuses/systems vital for assessing them.

While a few creators trust that, on account of the mind boggling, dynamic and impalpable results of instruction, a target estimation of value is exceptionally troublesome or unthinkable (Tofte, 1993; Sayed, 1993), many view it as fundamental if quality change is to be observed (Seymour, 1992; Morris and Haigh, 1993; Burkhalter, 1993). The terms 'client' and 'market' have additionally met with opposition from a few educationalists, who contend that they are pertinent just to business situations (Sallis, 1993; Corts, 1992). While understudies are prime clients of schools and colleges, they are additionally their crude material, providers, co-processors, and items" (Harris, 1992). For this, an elucidation is essential for determining clients and organizing or accommodating their distinctive necessities in light of a college mission (Taylor and Hill, 1993).

While a few overseers think that its hard to acknowledge the possibility of understudies as purchasers, truly, that is the thing that they are. In the present aggressive commercial center, schools are vendor offering course, a degree, and a rich graduate class life. Understudies are purchaser who enlist for course, apply for commencement, and make gifts as graduate class. The more haggard out these continuous exchanges are fit to the two get-together, the more comprehensive the association will development forward, to the upside of everybody (Bejou, 2005).

Course scrutinizing creation orders BSchools in the "not salary driven" association gathering, movements by B-Schools displays something other than what's expected. Bit of the pie, intense examination, orchestrating, and client driven association transport were contemplations held for the trade zone and were not of note to the breathing space of front line leadership (Kotler and Fox, 1995).

In spite of the way that not conveyed unequivocally, there is a stretching out structure among B-Schools to believe understudies to be clients. Understudies are clients and results of getting ready (Conway and Yorke, 1991)

An test facilitated by Delucci and Korgen (2002)48 for person discipline understudies, with a obsession review, demand that understudies believe that front line preparing capacities as a buyer driven business center. In the event that understudies are overseen as clients, are we trading off on the sweeping, generally speaking great conditions (remarkable citizenship, evident ability, moral attributes, essential limits, and so on) of B-

School getting ready, with brief, at the present time understudy focuses of compensating work .

Carlson and Fliesher (2002) opine, "This review of the understudy dead body as clients has abridged the careful natural world of the educational module and instruct events". In a student client introduction, it is firm to depict the "obsession", it could be receiving ready, yet this is a difficult structure in malice of for teacher, let alone for understudies (Clayson and Haley, 2005).

Clayson and Haley (2005) fight that analysis understudies as consumers is unseemly and has unenthusiastic impact on the understudy's enlightening welfare. The indication of this understudy as foreword has certain dramatic impacts like temporary viewpoint or a "clear An"- understudies may choose those course, where educator give basic evaluations and spotlight is on accomplish grades as opposed to genuine learning. Nonappearance of understudy responsibility Students may exchange duty of taking in and results of gaining from themselves to specialist organizations (B-School and workforce).

In an understudy client display, the item isn't promptly identifiable. It could be "instruction," however this is a tricky build notwithstanding for instructors, let alone for understudies if "training" is an item, at that point the client ought to have the capacity to get it either with cash or exertion. A degree might be viewed as simply one more product to be acquired (Emery et al. 2001).

Belohav (1984) proposes two perspectives; one to regard as the understudy as the next client and instant to consider control and big business areas as a convincing customers. Direction is a respect included system, the understudy is the exact opposite thing and the establishment is a storing up alliance,

The understudy can be measured as a communitarian instructive frill (Bay and Daniel, 2001: Henning-Thurau et al 2001). Ring and Emery (1971) and Fieldman (1971) wished-for the 'societal propelling beginning which underlines that an alliance exists to not just speak to its very own issues and the supplies of the client, yet despite keep up and advance people's and society's entire arrangement interests. Under this model, the point of confinement of a school or school is advance the wellbeing and objectives of understudies, workers, staff, watchmen, administration, and the general populace all things considered.

While understudy needs are focal in this introduction, a reasonable electorate far outflanks the understudies' concise needs and needs (Clayson and Haley, 2005). Groccia (1997)has deciphered the understudy as "an ensured understudy" by brightness of which, an understudy changes into a maker and not a purchaser, of the learning the individual being referred to increments.

The principal thought behind client work obligations is that at any rate clients are essentially energetic about the use of an association, when their abilities orchestrate those required to satisfy an undertaking required by the link, the coalition ought to utilize the clients' aptitude, making them "incomplete legislative body" (Mills and Morris, 1986).

This outlook of clients (or understudies) as halfway employees propose that they can and ought to be oversee as HR of an organization (Halbesleben, Becker, Buckley, 2003)

As per Laskey (1998), an informative association can take no beneath three of perspective on its guideline target of training understudies

Make national as-thing for society-as-client

Make laborer as-thing for supervisor as-client

Give personal growth associations as-thing for understudy as-client

As appeared by Sharrok (2000)63 on some unpredictable day, an understudy may be:
1. A client requiring routine data (from a division or staff office),
2. A customer requiring master heading (picking a course, or investigating a task),
3. A national with express rights (acquiring a book or interfacing with against a show of division), and
4. A subject with articulate duty (being fined for a long-ago due book, or wearisome to make a study)

Armstrong (2003) endorses 'the understudy's as-customer shows' customers who pay to get proficient associations from that firm. A customer is a man who draws in the ace guidance or associations of another.

The contact of an outline calm by Pitman (2000) on "feeling of managerial Staff towards student and sense" display so as to in managing understudies, authoritative staff have a tendency to relate intently to understudies, seeing them as inside clients. A partner who has a personal stake in obtaining advanced education. Understudy's needs will be given most extreme need by personnel in all parts of educational modules outline and conveyance. Personnel will be an official choice producer, by excellence of procured learning and important genuine experience (Shahaida, Rajashekar and Nargundkar, 2006) A comparative finding was found in an examination led by Obermiller, Fleenor and Raven (2005) where in insight and Preferences of undergrad and mark off understudies towards two foreword Students as clientele or crop was ended. The understudies favored the two introductions – client or item nearly the same. Experimental research around there is uncertain yet surviving writing survey demonstrates that more BSchools regard understudies as Customers.

Spanbauer (1995) brings up an extremely relevant issue, who is the instruction expected to profit? Understudies are essential clients yet the client relationship is to some degree not quite the same as a client in an eatery or bank. In both the mechanical and general administration segments, the clients are very much characterized though in a college, as

Madu and Kuei (1993) propose, the meaning of clients is very wide. While understudies are acknowledged as the essential clients by numerous creators (Sallis, 1993; Corts, 1992; Hittman, 1993), other potential clients, similar to guardians, businesses, government and society, ought to be considered. While considering nature of B-School training, it is important to consolidate the desires for some partners, understudies, personnel, government, managers, top managerial staff, society and so forth. The TQM reasoning focuses on constantly surpassing clients' desires, In advanced education, particularly B-Schools, which have numerous partners to fulfill, applying TQM like procedures (like in assembling industry) appears to be unreasonable. "The quantity of establishments that have really executed TQM effectively in any important way is nearly little, and the increases produced in these organizations frequently give off an impression of being eclipsed when and exertion" (Koch and Fisher, 1998)

Quality is hard to execute and catch in an important sense. Given the powers that place extreme, some of the time clashing weights on the supplier of MBA program, it winds up official upon us to believe about what excellence income in this day and age. (Rapert et al, 2004)

Studies directed in U.S.A advanced education foundations have demonstrated blended reaction about the viability of embracing TQM (Total Quality Management)- type quality procedures. An investigation of 32 advanced education foundations found that overseers trusted that their TQM program were building an strange commitment to hierarchical feasibility, and advantages were more prominent than costs (Elmutti and Manippillili, 1999).

Out of the 32 advanced education foundations, 12 establishments had abandoned TQM programs following a multi-year trail, refering to reasons, for example, hindering impacts on innovativeness, dangers of institutionalization and consistency and absence of suitable prizes. Not very many establishments have definitively made an accomplishment of actualizing TQM programs (Koch and Fischer, 1998).

Despite different issues associated with the execution of TQM– compose programs, numerous advanced education foundations are utilizing it to enhance scholastic organization, instructing and learning. The AACSB is supporting the utilization of constant process change projects to enhance educating and learning (Vazzana, Elfrink and Bachmann, 2001).

Koch and Fisher (1998) express that TQM has little to add to the arrangement of major inquiries of significant worth, course and asset distribution. TQM can be of help with enhancing authoritative administration zones (enrollment, mail benefit, support, charging, and so on.), and that it has been utilized to improve certain semi scholarly regions, for example, library administrations

Montmore and Stone (1990) opine that industry's view about reason for training is to deliver graduates who can impart, collaborate, take care of issues and work in a group viably. The understudy sees reason for training as a way to enhance profit and further profession prospects. The administration's viewpoint about reason for training might be to upgrade total understudy accomplishment.

Wicks (1992) propose different reasons for training, for example, securing of learning, constructing an esteem framework in the person, against which to make individual, social and good judgments and so forth. Personnel may see giving subject information and sharpening the calculated abilities of the understudies as the motivation behind training. The governing body perspective of reason for instruction could be three overlap to ingrain a feeling of order, to give successful instructing and to give great foundation and so on. The suppositions of different partners are assorted and furthermore exceedingly emotional

Montmore and Stone (1990) propose that there is nobody dimensional proportion of value and it is conceivable to talk about the nature of various segments of instruction
Adam smith alluded to nature of instructing as nature of training. Smith's idea of instructive quality sticks to customer's impression of value, J. S. Factory challenged this supposition, who called attention to that customers of instructive administration are frequently uninformed about the nature of the administration they are purchasing (Bose, 2006).

Bose (2006) contends nature of training given by to benefit and non-benefit suppliers of instruction is extraordinary. The assets accessible to a foundation can likewise be a measure for nature of instruction. Regardless of whether the organization is government subsidized or private supported affects both, the nature of training and the educational cost expenses charged. For government-financed foundations, the strain to expand number of understudies and fulfill the inclinations of the middle voter is less extreme. Understudies' accomplishments amid the course (positions, grants) and after the course (situations, proficient achievement) may likewise be considered as another marker of nature of training rendered in the establishment.

Epple and Romano (1998) and Basu (1989) suggest that a superior companion quality infers unrivaled quality as guaranteed by 'understudies' accomplishments. Benefit amplifying conduct decides nature of a school as evaluated by its associate quality (Basu, 1989). A benefit augmenting school picks the nature of understudies, to augment benefit. Purchasers ought to will pay a higher cost if a school is putting forth better quality.

Rothschild and White (1995) express that this sort of value separation disguises the externality that cunning poor and unremarkable rich understudies make inside the school. Accepting that state funded schools concede all understudies, subsequently government isn't worried about the nature of state funded schools, as long as they give instruction,

Epple and Romano (1998) attest that benefit amplifying schools will be of better quality. This statement has not been demonstrated experimentally. There are numerous non profit maximizing schools which are of better quality both in India and in addition different parts of the world. Research around there isn't significant to touch base at any important ends.

The main methodology takes after the administration's point of view and different analysts, for example, Sahney et al (2006), Brown, Keonig and Harold (1993), Davis and Allen (1990) Mahapatra and Khan (2007) have tried administration quality in advanced education foundations: Engineering and B-Schools. These specialists have utilized changed SERVQUAL scale proposed by Parasuraman, Zeithmal and Berry, (1985).

The second methodology receives the aggregate quality administration approach. Different Universities and B-Schools in U.S.A and U. K have embraced TQM compose approaches since the 1980's. Specialists, for example, Garvin (1984) and Burkhalter (1993) Morris and Haigh (1993), Spanbauer (1995), Owlia and Aspinwall (1998), Scrabec (2000), Widrick, Mergen and Grant (2002) have inquired about TQM in advanced education. Distinctive models have been recommended to enhance quality utilizing TQM.

The third methodology recommends utilizing the adjusted score card system to enhance quality in B-Schools. The adjusted score card is a strategy recommended by Kaplan and Norton (1996) for estimating execution in business associations.

As per Kaplan and Norton (2001), money related measures are slacking pointers of real hierarchical execution and recommend a methodology that holds monetary measures yet includes measures "on the drivers, the lead markers, of future budgetary execution" (Kaplan and Norton, 2001) Drtina, Gilbert and Alon (2007) have investigate the probability of apply the Balanced Score Card (BSC) to gauge quality in B-Schools.

The adjusted scorecard offers an approach to close the circle between key arranging and Business College rehearses with the goal that the key administration framework will drive hierarchical changes (Conger and Xin, 2000).

The key arranging process joins a frameworks approach, binds an association's central goal to representatives by giving successive input on every day activities. Before an association can actualize adjusted scorecard, it must characterize its methodology and its arrangement for the best approach to contend. The client offer is vital to this procedure since it characterizes the focused on clients and how the association will draw in and hold them (Drtina, Gilbert and Alon (2007).

The worldwide administration instruction advertise is evaluated to be US $22 billion (Friga, Bettis and Sullivan, 2003). It is creation at approximately 10-12 percent for each annum. U.S.A is the best marketplace. Around 900 American university obtainable an administrator degree in industry (Pfeffer and Fong 2002).The principal bunch of Harvard Business School graduates go out in 1945. By 1980, the outer condition of advanced education foundations including B-Schools began changing in the U.S.A. advanced education was confronting similar difficulties of the business world. Evolving socioeconomics, declining government bolster, quickly evolving innovation, developing prerequisites of responsibility by authorizing establishments and upgraded global rivalry for understudies, staff and research bolster were the real difficulties confronted (Lozier and Teeter, 1996)

The University of Pennsylvania directed a survey of business instruction in 1931. The report expressed that schools of business ought to set up a veritable control to be sound (Mc Farland, 1960) In 1959, the Carnegie Foundation drew out a provide details regarding administration instruction (Pierson, 1959). This report expressed that schools of business have neglected to distinguish and build up a veritable order portrayed by its very own assortment of topic, its very own hypothetical issues, its own examination and its very own procedures. It recommended that subdisciplines ought to develop, prompting specialization. Administration resources ought not stick too nearly to the recorded customs of the logical administration development.

The Gordon and Howell report {1959) depicted American business direction as "a gathering of exchange schools without a solid reasonable establishment" (Zimmerman, 2001)Emphasis was laid on giving all encompassing training, joining generalist and master learning. Doorman and Mc Kibbin (1988) noticed that business college educational module were viewed as excessively centered around examination, with lacking accentuation on issue finding as diverged from critical thinking and usage (Leavitt, 1986)

"We have constructed a strange, relatively unfathomable plan for MBA-level training" that contort those subjected to it into "critters with unstable brains, frosty heart, and slight spirits" (Leavitt, 1989 Various corporate colleges have in this way come up (Bowender and Rao, 2005). In 1982, AACSB and EFMD comprised an examination known as "Chiefs for the XXI Century" which suggested seven noteworthy rules for administration foundations. Establishments must create experiential courses in imagination, administrative advancement and build up a nearby association with honing chiefs (Bowender and Rao, 2005)

Two noteworthy examinations were directed in United Kingdom: the helpful report and Constable and McCormick report. These reports featured the requirement for qualified staff and the significance of preparing, worrying on connecting learning with individual and hierarchical objectives. Friga, Bettis and Sullivan (2003) have chronicled the example of US B-School development The discussion on the job of MBA restarted in US in 1990. (Hasan, 1993) announced that business colleges picked progressively to train what they wish to, as opposed to what business associations require. About two many years of scholastic business college examine had yielded practically zero basic information pertinent for the administration of contemporary or future business associations.

Business schools were allowed to pick any mission they needed as long as they archived the advancement towards accomplishing the mission. Yunker suggests that AACSB ought to elucidate the norms formally and after that base the accreditations in like manner (Yunker, 2000). Accreditation has made business colleges measure learning aptitudes and this had prompted ceaseless change. Research profitability must be a basic component of accreditation as it will actuate personnel to learn and advance. One of the reactions of accreditation process is that schools with customer relationship and generally are not separated. It wound up obvious that wide basing accreditation, and making levels inside, might be the best system for constant change. Different levels of projects should utilize distinctive measuring sticks, for example, showing adequacy, investigate efficiency, customer relationship and oddity of projects (Bowender and Rao, 2005)

The significance of value administration training d oes not go unrecognized. For instance, the Global Competitiveness Index, made yearly by the World Economic Forum, joins as a variable the possibility of a country's association schools. The World Bank in like way utilizes countries' scores on this variable as a touch of its Knowledge Assessment Methodology (KAM), which encourages countries distinguish intends to change to a knowledge based economy

As per Dr. Chakravarthy An: A business college is typically a university level foundation that shows subjects, for example, bookkeeping, back, promoting, hierarchical conduct, vital arranging, quantitative strategies, and so on. These incorporate schools of "business", "business organization", and "administration". It should likewise make understudies mindful of utilization programming, for example, ERP, POS, Simulation, SCM and coordination's. Notwithstanding this they should likewise get the opportunity to learn of the genuine running of an undertaking. A business college is a substance by itself and cannot be kept running as a branch of a specialized school now.

Indian B-Schools are extensively named:

1. Self-governing B-Schools which are associated to Ministry of HRD and AICTE, for example, Indian Institutes of Managements, Xavier's Labor Relations Institute Jamshedpur, S P Jain Institute of managing and Research Mumbai, Xavier's

Institute of Management Bhubaneswar, Fore School of Management, Delhi and so on.

2. Administration schools and offices in colleges go under the domain of national college training framework. They are controlled and checked by University Grants Commission (UGC). Focal Universities are observed by UGC and state colleges are checked by state governments and mostly by UGC.
3. College Affiliated Colleges are guided by University principles and controls.
4. Private Universities supported by social orders/trusts/corporate bodies are guided by UGC.

As indicated by Dr. Ashutosh Priya (2006), there are different purposes behind the colossal development of B-Schools in India. There have be basic and irreversible changes in the financial system, government approach, standpoint of business and business, and in the approach of the Indians as a rule.

From a deficiency economy of nourishment and outside trade, India has now turned into a surplus one. From an agro-based economy, India has developed as an administration arranged one. From the low-development of the past, the economy has turned into a high-development one in the long haul. Having been a guide beneficiary, India is presently joining the guide providers club In spite of the fact that India was late and moderate in modernization of industry as a rule in the past, it is currently a leader in the rising Knowledge based New Economy The Government is proceeding with its change and progression not out of impulse but rather out of conviction.

Indian organizations are not any more perplexed of Multinational company. They have become all wide-ranging aggressive and a considerable lot of them have moved toward becoming MNCs themselves. Indian administration graduates never again line up for safe government employments. They favor and appreciate the difficulties and dangers of getting to be business visionaries and worldwide players in the rising private divisions.

SERVICE QUALITY AND INSTITUTION'S QUALITY

Organization transcendence is portrayed as "the capability between customers' prospect for organization routine going before the organization find and their impression of the organization accepted" (Asubonteng et al 1996) while the alleged organization worth is described as "an overall end, or assessments, relating to the pro of the examination" (Parasuraman et. al. 1988). There are eight degree of significant worth that include execution, skin, steady quality, conformance, quality, organization office, feel and saw unmistakable quality (Garvin 1987). The shallow organization worth totally explains the worth viewpoint in organizations industry (Reeves and Bednar 1994) and this is additional supported by Gruber et al. (2010) who quarrel that higher learning is mainly intangible, unpreserved and varied, resulting in aspect of the service knowledge varying from one state of affairs to after that and making them hard to evaluate. Sultan and Wong (2010) stated that repair quality should be seen as background issues since its size vary womanishly. Lovelock and Wirtz (2011) believed that excellence means dissimilar things to dissimilar people depending on the context being examine, and that two citizens can have radically different perception of the same check.

There are 19 different service quality model available in the there literature (Seth et.al. 2005). These model include:

(1) Technical and handy quality representation (Gronroos 1984);

(2) Service eminence gap copy (Parasuraman et al 1985);

(3) Attribute tune-up quality sculpt (Haywood-Farmer 1988);

(4) Synthesised replica of service excellence (Brogowicz et al 1990);

(5) Performance only replica (Cronin and Taylor 1992);

(6) Ideal value replica of seragainstice quality (Mattsson 1992);

(7) Evaluated presentation and normed quality model (Teas 1993);

(8) IT position model (Berkley and Gupta 1994);

(9) Attribute and on the whole affect mock-up (Dabholkar 1996);

(10) Model of seeming service value and fulfillment (Spreng and Mackoy 1996);

(11) PCP power model (Philip and Hazlett 1997);

(12) Retail repair quality and apparent value replica (Sweeney, Soutar and Johnson 1997);

(13) Service quality, purchaser value and customer approval model (Oh 1999);

(14) Antecedents and go-between model (Dabholkar et al 2000);

(15) Internal renovate quality mock-up (Frost and Kumar 2000);

(16) Internal service distinction DEA model (Soteriou and Stavrinides 2000);

(17) Internet bank mock-up (Broderick and Vachirapornpuk 2002);

(18) IT-based shape (Zhu et al 2002), and

(19) Model of e-service quality (Santos 2003)..

Among the a variety of overhaul quality model, the two nearly everyone commonly quoted service eminence models are the work and functional class copy (Gronroos 1984) and the Service distinction gap model, also recognized as SERVQUAL copy (Parasuraman et. al. 1985). There are five key scale of the SERVQUAL model which canister be used by customers to appraise insight of the in general apparent repair quality. These scope built-in reliability, statement, tangibles, receptivity and considerate (Parasuraman et. al. 1988). The SERVQUAL copy is usually used and take on in the extant symbols to evaluate the full as a whole students' theoretical service worth in the education manufacture (Russell 2005). The SERVQUAL mock-up that is town by (Parasuraman et al 1985) is specially made by researchers to count 'the gap between customers expected level of mend and their approaching of the actual service' (Bennett et al 2003) in gauge the determinants of obvious service quality of educational institutions. In a study by data unperturbed from the American College annoying program, Krampf and Heinlein (1981) establish that eventual student who have a optimistic feelings toward the institute of higher teaching rated the pleasant look of the campus, enlightening campus visits, recommendation of relations, good program in their main, enlightening college catalogue, proximity to home and the directness of the campus impression as significant determinants in their favorite for the institute.

Cook and Zallocco (1983) opined that word of lips recommendation from family and friends constitute a major basis of influence on students' institution of higher education choice. Intangibility, the lack of bodily evidence for a repair, forces a customer to rely on sources of in sequence such as speech of mouth recommendation to arrive at purchase decisions. Specifically, a future student gathers in order from others who have attend or attending the organization, parents, associates, relatives etc concerning a higher education organization and form an expectation about the excellence of service he be supposed to receive from the organization. Other source of in order such as institutional advertisement and institution of higher education guides will also crash on choice of institution of higher education by student.

Table 2.1 Attributes of quality in product/service models (TQM) with quality education (TQE)

Total Quality Management	Total Quality Education
Performance	Student performance
Features	Degree options, courses
Reliability	Capabilities and skills developed
Conformance	Conformance to national, state and professional standards
Durability	Marketability of learned skills/knowledge
Service ability	Ability to meet professional requirements and accreditation
Perceived Quality	Contribution to improving society

In an examination to approach about the school decision framework for optional school understudies, the Carnegie basis (1986) audit revealed that train divisions, grounds visits, right pass school advocates, next of kin educators for college and convention with school director were the the largest part on an crucial estimation elementary factors in the school decision configuration. In looking morsel of criticalness of an assortment of individuals in the school sale process, the Carnegie do research found that gate keeper (32%), mates (14%), instructor (9%), and educator, (9%) inclined the understudies. In an extra inspection looking variety key association among understudies in Dallas province Texas group of people College, Massey (1997) found that the main thing expert technique relied upon effects from gatekeepers (77%), mates (54%), optional educators (31%), family (30.5%) and accomplice school guides (24%).

Bitner (1990, 1992) demonstrates the veracity of that the physical workplaces can display the inspirations driving constrainment and the quality vacant by the consent based friendship. The bodily workplaces of the tertiary coalition all around do impact the general understudies' sensible alliance quality since understudies will interface express authentic bits with the affiliations given by the moved direction establishment (Oldfield and Baron 2000; Russell 2005). Understudies who put in hours constantly in a school are likely going to have points of view towards the illuminating structure that are unequivocally impacted by the physical workplaces (Wakefield and Blodgett 1994).

An examination of green beans demand at Washington State University using the accreditation working conditions 'vivacious pushing toward understudy structure', an online affirmation contraption, found that production occasion after commencement, get-together of course, course cost, staff name, unequivocal illuminating activities, occupation coordinating, school reputation and cabin openings were the key bits impacting their choice (Sanders 1986). Another examination in like manner found that understudies' option of a major be affected by a family demonstrate up than by an sore to go to a specific basis (Dixon and Martin 1991).

Ramden (1991) pummeled the essential associate pointers with check the appearing in front line engineering through the survey procedure and influenced that the instructor's examination experience and the drawing in framework they handle are the goliath presentation markers.

Sevier's (1993) consider on option of school by African-Americans establish that the alternative of school was exaggerated by reputation of school, receptiveness of budgetary guide, stanch cost of visiting, work place record, and natural world of staff, geographic zone, and figure of understudies. As showed up by McDonnell (1995), there were eight territories contemplated when considering school choice. Those parts are illuminating reputation, size of school, a land zone, selectivity of school, cash related guide straightforwardness, shrewd program responsiveness, understudy loads and social air.

An test of the parts that prejudiced universal understudies' choice of go objective in Australia by Mazzarol et al (1996) establish that the most middle explanation factor was the make sure of their capacity by future business, establishment standing for quality, its capacity to see precedent cutoff focuses and the staff reputation for superiority and quality.

Lin's (1997) separate on the clarifications following understudies' pick of a lighting up relationship in The Netherlands, using vanity audits that were self-genuinely scattered to understudies in the parlor zones of seven Universities revealed that the most boss purposes behind an understudy's choice of establishment was preparing offered, calling openings, the school's reputation, open segment for brief business, workforce limits, instructive measures, paying little character to whether current workplaces were available, enlightening technique supplement, understudy life among others, etc were the parts that impacted their choice of the foundation.

The bodily workplaces of the tertiary establishment had been attempted by various experts in the present sythesis as one of the mammoth determinants of the general understudies' undeniable association quality (LeBlanc and Nguyen 1997; Ford et. al. 1999; Sohail and Shaikh 2004; Joseph et. al. 2005).

Mario Rapso Helena Alves (1998) passed on that the affiliation needs are changed by three significant zones a) Learning and business b) Reputation and workplaces of the school c) Availability and empathy of the staff. Wetzel et al (1999) got a couple of data about the parts influencing understudy's satisfaction and found that an ideal school level mate, changing as shown by another social condition, reputation of the foundation and the ability to progress through the smart program affected satisfaction.

Scrabec (2000) has provided splendid quality guidance model subject to central spotlights and on quality managing properties. The model showed understudy satisfaction in setting on complete quality arranging technique, yet not the focal examination to improve the structure. This model related with understudy examinations to be a dash of the general structure. The model used inside looking improve the system structure dependably. As showed up by Scrabec (2000), the TQE model is totally closer to truth of the odd thought unquestionably, not in the most unassuming degree like the TQM replica where facilitators use appraisal as the show examination circle, ousting the terminations and fundamental for the beneficiaries (society, industry, watches and purposes for living). Scarbec (2000) in like way opined that to operationalize the bits of in order of TQM to quality in arrange is gravely overseen. He proposed eight potential degrees of fundamental worth heading; they are managed national tests, referencing of instructive affiliations, understudy satisfaction measures, industry input, unending substance and quantitative measures, national records, for instance, licenses, relationship of self-choice examinations to set benchmarks and understudies examinations.

Widrick, Mergen and Grant (2002) have investigated three quality estimations (nature of plan, nature of conformance and nature of execution) in bleeding edge organizing. They have built up a huge amount of estimation parameters utilized in taking a gander at examination and illuminating structure headway and instruments/frameworks significant for exploring them.

Gupta, Gollakota and Sreekumar (2003) have proposed five checks to quantify nature of the boss bearing in India. They are,

(I) Quality of understudies including the attestation method,

(ii) Pedagody,

(iii) Placement

(iv) Faculty headway and

(v) Infrastructure.

Bearing is an affiliation direct showed up by the provider. Pushed heading foundations are setting always clear update on get-together understudy needs and needs. As, Universities and higher edifying foundations continue influencing the opportunity to be insignificant understudy overseen. Understudy perspective on higher illuminating workplaces and affiliations are reshaping up understandably basic. Coalition quality in bleeding edge bearing underlining understudy satisfaction is a beginning late making field of stress in the Universities and establishments.

Rao (2006) has proposed a model for achieving suffering quality improvement and rule talking standards for the board informational establishments. The parameters of the proposed model are,

(I) Academic instructive game-plan benchmarking, responsiveness and bearing to moving corporate needs,

(ii) Internal checking

(iii) Leadership and institutional coalition,

(iv) International affiliations and diagrams

(v) Global accreditations and brief positions

(vi) Benchmarking for all around accreditation.

Sahney, Banwet and Karunes (2006) drove a cautious examination using SERVQUAL estimations. The reason behind mix of the examination was on watching a structure of plan credits formed to suit quality in course and went for seeing and working up linkages and association between the customer fundamentals (understudies of Engineering and Management) and the structure characteristics. The examination studied the solicitation and fundamental for understudies for both the customer basics and structure properties.

Mahapatra and Khan (2007) built up a scale called 'EduQUAL' having 43 things drawn from SERVQUAL and various examinations. The scale was made to understudies, graduated class, watchmen of understudies and choice executives of different express establishments transversely over India. Factor examination demonstrated imperative alpha traits for the going with estimations: learning results, responsiveness, physical workplaces, character improvement and scholastics.

Babar Zaheer Butt and Kashif Ur Rehman (2010) investigated the determinants of understudies' satisfaction in bleeding edge getting ready and found that teacher's capacity, courses offered, learning condition and study door working situations improve the understudies' satisfaction. The examination moreover given that instructive condition unquestionably was the crucial factor in picking edifying establishments. Informational condition gathers library working situations, journals open, PC working conditions and alike.

David Wetcher and Neves (2003) found illuminating and quality concerning instructing in the subject had less effect on everything considered understudy satisfaction and confirmation while extracurricular activities, calling openings and nature of planning were the fragments with sensibly tremendous impact on understudies' satisfaction.

The physical workplaces of the tertiary establishment subject to the examination of Sohail and Shaikh (2004) set the procedure of the examination regions, the lighting in the homerooms, the closeness of the grounds structures and ground, the settlement of access to the ending office, PC office and study room office, the solace of the examination entries and study rooms, in end the profitability and cleanliness of the grounds. Deshields et al (2005) referenced the strong learning condition was dependably identified with the understudies' fulfillment.

The expense of courses offered had been tried by unequivocal stars in the suffering creation as one of the real determinants of the general understudies clear alliance quality (Hill 1995; Kennington et. al. 1996; Ford et. al. 1999; and Joseph et. al. 2005). The things in the expense of courses offered join get-together of stipends offered to understudies, paying little character to whether the expense of the instructive program was sensible at long last whether the unconstrained affiliation charges were sensible.

As appeared by the examination wrapped up by Ford et al (1999), reasonable cost of heading impacts the general understudies' unquestionable affiliation quality. Additionally, the system of cash related relationship, for instance, give was appeared to be one of the gigantic determinants of the general understudies' sensible association quality (Hill 1995).

Nandi D.K. (2010) drove an examination on 'Without inquiry Management Students' Expectations from B-Schools: An Empirical Analysis'. The data was amassed using audits among 100 certain association understudies who went to various masterminding relationship as status of their MBA check test in Ranchi and Jamshedpur in Jharkhand, India. The results exhibited that there exists strong relationship among's costs and understudies' satisfaction. Further structure the degree that anyone knows was the most affecting variable for the impressive MBA understudies in picking B-Schools.

The likelihood of affiliations was reflected in the endeavor that was finished by the specific master relationship through their relationship with the client during the time spent passing on such affiliations (Heskett 1987; Surprenant and Solomon 1987). This inquiry was kept up by Bitner et al. (1990). The human assistance piece will affect the customer's examination structure in inquiring about the sensible affiliation quality (Bitner et al., 1990). As shown by Sohail and Shaikh (2004), contact workforce was seen as one of the free factors for the general understudies' certain association quality. The contact work control reliant on the examination of Sohail and Shaikh (2004) join sensibility, thought and respect showed up by the heads; thought and sympathy showed up by the speakers; precision and deliberateness of the teachers; most remote ranges of the workforce to play out their duties fittingly; and sponsorship of records by the controllers.

The association quality was generally seen by the endeavor of the hard and fast staff and informative staff of the establishment. A tremendous proportion of the understudies has de-induced when they found that the staff was not careful and kind. As demonstrated by Hasan et al (2008), for quality check a foundation must train its staff people with an indisputable spotlight on that it may make an evaluation of help by systems for coordination, joint effort, compassion and empathy.

In light of the examinations of Sanders (1986); Dixon and Martin (1991); Sevier (1993); McDonnell (1995); Mazzarol et al (1996); Kennington et al (1996); Lin (1997); Sohail and Shaikh (2004); and Joseph et al (2005):six free factors were found colossal for the present examination to be unequivocal

(1) Access to workplaces;

(2) Academics;

(3) Physical workplaces of the tertiary establishment;

(4) Reputation of the establishment;

(5) Cost of courses offered; and

(6) Contact work control.

SERVICE QUALITY AND STUDENTS' SATISFACTION

A few examinations had demonstrated that an odd state of client association quality could apply an obliging outcome on buyer consistency (Cronin and Taylor 1992). Arrangement quality was in like way noted as a fundamental thing for structure up and supporting fulfilling association with respected clients. In like way, the relationship between alliance quality and buyer perseverance had made as a subject of key and key concern. While association quality was a general assessment of the relationship under thought, customer duty was a marker of unequivocal affiliation exchanges. Regardless, little was thought concerning the alliance quality discernments in India (Jain and Gupta 2004) as most examinations had been done inside the establishment of made nations (Herbig and Genestre 1996).

Seen affiliation quality is a pioneer to fulfillment (Spreng and Mackoy 1996). In like way, a fitting impression of the pioneers and determinants of purchaser determination could be viewed as to have an astoundingly high budgetary inspiration for association relationship in a related with space (Lassar et. al. 2000). The standard association quality research had been other than revived through work in the space of customer obligation (Spreng et. al. 1996; Oliver 1997). Kotler and Clarke (1987) depicted fulfillment as the standard unavoidable consequence of an undertaking or work that satisfies one's regard. As per Zeithaml (1988), fulfillment was the resultant given up delayed consequence of an establishment's regulatory additionally as illuminating structure's reasonable execution. Understudy's fulfillment proposes the beneficial thought of an understudy's stunning assessment of the results and encounters related with bearing (Oliver and DeSarbo 1989). Understudy fulfillment had been shaped reliably by underscored encounters in grounds life. In like manner, the grounds condition was clearly a catch of interconnected encounters that checked and influenced understudy's general fulfillment (Elliott and Shin 2002). High alliance quality expanded buyer unwaveringness which accomplished high client devotion and essentialness to course to different people (Bolton and Drew 1991; Boulding 1993; Rust 1994; Nadiri and Hussain 2009).

Oliver (1993) battled that clients experienced nature of things or affiliations so as to pick whether they are fulfilled or not. In this line, connection quality was showed up contrastingly in relationship with the likelihood of examination, and fulfillment changed into a stacked with loving idea. Most examinations had considered alliance quality as the pioneer of customer obligation (Fornell 1992; Anderson et. al. 1994; Fornell et. al. 1996; Cronin et. al. 2000).

Bearden and Teel (1983); Cadotte, Woodruff and Jenkins (1987), observationally researched subject to the throbbing disconfirmation hypothesis that, purchasers structure fulfillment decisions by assessing veritable execution against their prepurchase demand regarding the thing. Quickly, clients structure suppositions concerning a thing subject to their establishing with the thing or an in each reasonable sense not all around portrayed thing, word-ofmouth recommendations and maker's progressing. This hankering filled in as a stay for coming about post buy evaluation. An examination between the hankering and veritable use experience would result in fulfillment if execution thrashings needs or blocked need if execution affirmations fall underneath necessities.

Athiyaman (1997) empowered an examination with 1432 understudies from different piece of forefront course in Australia. The examination expected to discover the connection between watched quality and customer pledge. The outcome exhibited that there was a high association between's understudy fulfillment and saw excellence measures.

Soutar and McNeil (1996) dissected 109 understudies in an Australian University and got some information about the connection between watched alliance quality and understudy fulfillment. The outcomes demonstrated that the understudy fulfillment was all around affected by the specific affiliation quality estimations that had a relationship with the lighting up areas. Further, Yunus et al (2010) maintained an examination among 200 understudies in 4 Malaysian Polytechnic foundations to test the connection between inspiration, supporting, and alliance quality towards understudies' fulfillment. The examination results exhibited that inspiration, propping, and connection quality were impacting understudies' fulfillment. In like way, it other than demonstrated that association quality was the most impacting parts towards understudies' fulfillment.

Rust and Oliver (1994) endorsed that quality was subordinate to fulfillment; quality was one unequivocal association estimation in their fulfillment decisions. Bigne et al (2003) found that the general association quality had a principal association with fulfillment with R= 0.66. Ham and Hayduk (2003) had referenced that, even in the higher lighting up settings, there was a positive connection between's impression of association quality and understudies' fulfillment, and looking the relationship subject to a goliath bit of the bit of association quality, unsurprising quality (R=0.547; sig. = 0.000) had the most grounded relationship restricted for after by responsiveness and compassion (R=0.5431; sig. = 0.000), demand (R=0.492; sig. = 0.000) and substance (R=0.423; sig.= 0.000)

Estimations AND STUDENTS' SATISFACTION

Research totally demonstrates that suppositions related with affiliations could see a mammoth improvement in update fulfillment (Westbrook 1987; Dube Rioux 1990; Oliver 1993; Price et. al. 1995; Stauss and Neuhaus 1997; Liljander and Strandvik 1997; Wirtz and Bateson 1999). Obviously, Oliver (1996) illustrated fulfillment as 'a pleasurable piece of usage related satisfaction'. Bloemer and Ruyter (1999)correspondingly transmitted an impression of being changed structures for positive assessments make an astonishing delineation of the puzzling idea of fulfillment. As appeared by Bigne and Andreu (2004), the association experience influenced the period of customer slants, and those therefore influence purchaser duty and lead needs. As necessities be, client evaluative decisions depended about the entire workshop on idea and somewhat on related reactions to an alliance improvement.

Seeing how buyers felt about an interest experience had little an impacting power before long or speculation without a specific condition or result, and questions had been investigated in relationship with customer centrality (Westbrook and Oliver 1993), post-buy shapes (Dube and Menon 2000), understanding in including fulfillment decisions (Homburg et al 2006; Yu and Dean 2001), the craving for social targets (Ladhari 2007; Morris et al 2002), and collusion quality (Chiu and Wu 2002; Jiang and Wang 2006).

Dube and Menon (2000) found that positive and negative inclinations impacted fulfillment a positive and negative way wholeheartedly. In looking relationship among examinations and fulfillment showed diverse suggestion. They are: (1) perseveringly dazzling other-credited negative estimations will have a negative fulfillment; and (2) the relationship among condition and self-ascribed negative sentiments will be brilliantly connected with fulfillment. The first proposed negative relationship between other-credited negative propensities and fulfillment (Oliver 1993; Taylor and Baker 1994) and the second proposed positive relationship between self-ascribed negative proclivity and fulfillment (Schwarz and Clore 2003;White 2006) had gotten solid help recorded as a printed change. The positive relationship between positive terminations and fulfillment had in like way been all around recorded (Ladhari 2007; Oliver 1993; Yu and Dean 2001).

As showed up by attribution experts, negative terminations were settled by office clarification behind conviction or who were accountable for causing a terrible occasion, where oneself was seen as solid, emotions, for example, bending makes; where others were cautious, examinations, for example, spread, weight and bewilderment happens (Roseman 1996). To wrap up, (Positive/negative) feelings (really/dreadfully) affected fulfillment.

Keen DISSONANCE AND STUDENTS' SATISFACTION

The general point of view in fulfillment research clear fulfillment as a sensibly based examination of thing or affiliation execution (Yi 1990; Fournier and Mick 1999). Inquisitively, an improvement of moving examination on fulfillment had prescribed that fulfillment mixes a vivacious part, without which fulfillment can't be completely clarified (Westbrook and Oliver 1991; Oliver 1993; Oliver 1997; Fournier and Mick 1999; and Zeelenberg and Pieters 2004).

Sweeney et al. (1996), was the first to unequivocally check the relationship among sensible assortment from the standard and fulfillment. Sweeney et al. (1996) plot clients' heavenly and fulfillment levels following the buy and usage of electrical strong things. Working out as proposed to get-together the disharmony and fulfillment estimations and factor looking pooled things, the things investigating weight and fulfillment stacked onto two unequivocal makes. In a general sense more on a critical estimation, disharmony to the degree anybody knows was evidently identified with fulfillment when fulfillment was low yet wrecked back to it when fulfillment was high. Mission for after (1970) gutted disharmony over a pre-buy, post-buy use continuum. He found that driving cooler buyers who got post-regard based supporting from the store point by point lower disharmony levels and unfalteringly raising show toward the store. Further, Koller and Salzberger (2007) drew nearer about mental disharmony concerning the utilization of a get-together visit. It exhibited that disharmony was able about post-buy correspondingly as in the pre-buy and even in the pre-choice make.

The examination by O'Neil and Palmer (2004), utilizing a longitudinal structure over a one-month time bit found that modifications in school understudies' commotion over their decision of school oppositely identify with changes in the understudies' impression of the school's association quality. Parasuraman et al (1985) saw that raising experts started to conceptualize fulfillment as a flooding with preferring reaction to help, as opposed to a really based assessment of properties. Oliver (1989) all the more then likely overseen fulfillment to the degree five express modes – if its start and end the indistinguishable from you should control, trademark and daze. Fulfillment pros everything considered concur that fulfillment is completely picked significant acknowledgment (Yi 1990 and Oliver 1997). Thus, suffering examination on fulfillment would imagine that one's fulfillment level ought not be impacted by pieces unessential to utilize. Regardless, such sort of data can influence fulfillment through a twisting way. Zajonc (1980) fights that individuals will when all is said in done base their judgment of an article on contemplations they experience toward that object, and that the vitality of emotions is speedier and ceaselessly farsighted to coming about bits of data than the movement of reason based examinations of the thing. The focal reason covered the effect as-data theory is that inferable from the horrible and trademark nature of inquiries, individuals can't fundamentally watch the bases of their affinities, and they will with everything considered join such examinations into happening as arranged, totally unnecessary, approach of tendency and viewpoint game-plan (Schwarz and Clore 1983; Wyer et. al. 1999). Such an effect move impact is most empowered when coming about decisions are clearing and feelingsbased (Gorn 1982). In any case, the improvement of disunity does not prescribe that the two bits of inconvenience, the mental weight and worry over learning of decision, will influence fulfillment. On an unbelievably basic estimation mental uneasiness included connected with recognition and was everything seen as prepared for moving its stacked with getting a charge out of substance to fulfillment improvement. Difficult to miss, the psychological area of distress – the purchasers' worry over the fairness and information of decision – won't affect fulfillment. Along these lines, it was predicted that while the unequivocally hot bit of weight impacts fulfillment, the psychological piece of refinement did not influence fulfillment.

Wen Mao and Harmen Oppewal (2009) separated the impacts of post-buy fortress and decision conflicting data, the rest of which vitalizes related fight on buyer commitment and saw conspiracy quality (PSQ). A field test was driven in which school understudies were furnished with school rankings data that was either dependable with their decision of school or conflicting with their decision. It was discovered that approach of decision conflicting data impacts neither fulfillment nor saw association quality. Whimsically, while not influencing PSQ, approach of post-buy fortress improves fulfillment. The producer demonstrated this to result from a reducing stuck in an amazing condition concerning the decision made, which was the vivacious bit of tense battle.

STUDENTS' SATISFACTION AND ATTITUDE TOWARDS THE INSTITUTION

Client significant union system is a bewildering and clearing structure. Buyers survey the quality they get similarly as make tempers subject to the fulfillment felt by the affiliations got. In relationship with buyer relentlessness and habits, it had been discovered that fulfilled customers make positive brand viewpoints and brand affinities towards the article they were content with (Roest and Pieters 1977; Oliver 1980; Bolton 1998). Totally when fulfillment is treated as a post buy amass, the creation kept up the talk that the getting a charge out of or relative lifting point of view of the purchaser will be made subject to all around fulfilling use events of the alliance (Bearden and Teel 1983; Dick and Basu 1994; O'Cass and Grace 2004). Burton et al (2001) struggle that "a purchaser's general point of view got from the totality of their emotions ought to be reliant on their unyielding fulfillment, which will subsequently be affected by examinations subject to both direct understanding and data got from outside sources or signs".

As shown by Seymour (1993), the genuine reason for blend of cutting edge heading depended coming to fruition to making many fulfilled clients, for example, understudies, watchmen of understudies, graduated class, or industry business. In like way, concentrating on improving the client steadiness at schools and colleges was central in making client respect.

Understudies' qualitys would be appeared as positive or negative (Keaveney 1995) in light of how far understudies' needs on the automobile of the affiliation had been met by the association. On the off possibility that a negative conduct was molded, it is hard to accomplish standard talking fulfillment and could result in partitions, lessening responsibility and negative fulfilling development (Kau and Loh 2006; Maxham 2001). In light of the past examinations (Bitner 1990; Bolton and Drew 1991) understudies' fulfillment was considered as a pioneer to perspective in thi Research plainly shows that emotions related with affiliations could imagine a basic activity in influencing satisfaction (Westbrook 1987; Dube Rioux 1990; Oliver 1993; Price et. al. 1995; Stauss and Neuhaus 1997; Liljander and Strandvik 1997; Wirtz and Bateson 1999). Especially, Oliver (1996) plot fulfillment as 'a pleasurable zone of usage related satisfaction'.

Bloemer and Ruyter (1999)correspondingly appeared, apparently, to be different frameworks for positive assessments make a staggering arrangement of the diserse thought of satisfaction. As showed up by Bigne and Andreu (2004), the affiliation experience affected the time of buyer suppositions, and those in like way impact client satisfaction and social targets. Everything considered, customer evaluative choices depended about the whole workshop on affirmation and everything considered on braced responses to an alliance improvement.

Perceiving how customers felt about a connection experience had little a motivation over the long haul or speculation without an astounding condition or result, and suppositions had been explored in association with client continuing on quality (Westbrook and Oliver 1993), post-purchase shapes (Dube and Menon 2000), learning in obliging satisfaction choices (Homburg et al 2006; Yu and Dean 2001), the hankering for lead focuses (Ladhari 2007; Morris et al 2002), and association quality (Chiu and Wu 2002; Jiang in addition to Wang 2006).

Dube and Menon (2000) found that activist and negative supposition inclined discharge a positive and downbeat way eagerly. In examining the relationship among feelings and fulfillment indicated various suggestions. They are: (1) perseveringly sublime other-ascribed negative appraisals will have a unenthusiastic completion; and (2) the relationship in the middle of state and self-credited negative tendency will be truly associated with fulfillment. The first proposed negative relationship between other-ascribed negative evaluations and fulfillment (Oliver 1993; Taylor and Baker 1994) and the second proposed positive rapport between self-credited off-putting preference and achievement (Schwarz and Clore 2003; White 2006) had gotten strong assistance recorded as a printed change. The positive association between positive emotions and satisfaction had in like way been particularly low down (Ladhari 2007; Oliver 1993; Yu and Dean 2001).

As showed up by attribution authorities, negative thoughts were settled by relationship without a doubt or who were in charge of causing a disturbing event, where oneself was regarded fit, suppositions, for instance, imperfection makes; where others were attentive, inclines, for instance, trance, sharpness and frustration occurs (Roseman 1996). To wrap up, (Positive/negative) estimations (valiantly/forebodingly) affected satisfaction.s study.

ATTITUDE TOWARDS THE INSTITUTION AND BEHAVIOURAL OUTCOME

In client direct, there was a general accord that atmosphere impacts buyer social point (Fishbein and Ajzen 1975; Mackenzie and Lutz 1989). The key weakness for a goliath bit of the past temper lead research was that the improvement of moving quality would outfit disengaging behavior related and the way object (Griffin and O'Cass 2004). Perspective combined through unfathomably close experiences will reason behind reality envision direct than penchants ricochet through circumlocutory moving correspondence (Grace and O'Cass 2005; Fazio et. al. 1989).

Understudies may have mind blowing direct (FB) and unpleasant lead (UFB) towards an affiliation. FB could wires re-decision objective, plan of positive verbal, and progressing toward accomplices and relatives to apply for requesting; and UFB could cover might want to draw a little while later from school, methodology of negative astonishing, and crippling sidekicks and relatives to apply for arrangements. Boulding et al (1993), in an examination which included school understudies, saw strong association between connection quality and direct; and Ham (2003), in a work which included school understudies, found an essential connection between's quality, satisfaction and understudy obvious quality goals/challenges.

Concerning course, the focal results found by express experts were commitment, questions (Webb and Jagun 1997), and verbal exercises (Athiyaman 1997). An understudy trustworthy to his or her edifying establishment must have a positive mental and vivified path towards the foundation, one that gives the secured motivation to his or her direct (Hennig - Thurau T. et. al. 2001). Understudy imagination was a key fixation for some higher enlightening relationship as the upsides of the understudy commitment were not bound to the time that the understudy spends in the foundation. As appeared by Hennig-Thurau T. et al (2001), understudy responsibility spreads impelling behavior, for instance, (I) not too bad degrees of progression (ii) repurchasing objective (iii) referral needs and (iv) graduated class related focus interests.

As appeared by Ajzen and Fishbein (1980), individuals who had clearly evaluated the direct had strong should need to partake in lead what's constantly observed that the others ought to dissect that fast. Along these lines, this examination contemplates air towards establishment as the harbinger to lead result.

OVERALL SATISFACTION AND BEHAVIOURAL OUTCOME

Numerous empirical studies have reported that satisfaction was the predictor of behaviour outcomes (Cronin et. al. 2000; Olorunniwo et. al. 2006; Choi et. al. 2004). Zeithaml, Berry, and Parasuraman (1996) proposed that positive social result were reflected in specialist organizations' capacity to have clients (I) say positive things regarding them, (ii) prescribe them to different shoppers, (iii) stay faithful to them, (iv) go through more cash with them, and (v) pay cost premiums.

In the present setting, "past conduct" speaks to the instructive encounters with the college; and these instructive encounters will clearly initiate training fulfillment as fulfillment was characterized as an evaluative synopsis of utilization experience, in light of the disparity between earlier desires and genuine execution saw following utilization (Tse and Wilton 1988). As fulfillment catches a subjective nature of past practices as an evaluative outline of utilization experience, it was probably going to directly affect aims. The immediate positive impact of fulfillment on expectation was likewise observationally approved by Bitner (1990) and Chen et. al. (2009).

Fulfilling utilization encounters benefits buyers, organizations and social orders (Anderson et al 1994; Fornell et al 1996) and had been recognized to prompt positive verbal (Bearden and Teel 1983), more elevated amounts of brand faithfulness (Mittal and Kamakura 2001) and rehashed buy aims (Westbrook 1987). Taylor and Cronin (1994), in his examination found that there was a moderate to solid connection between the consumer loyalty and buyer unwaveringness or continue obtaining conduct. Richins (1983) in his examination broke down that negative word-ofmouth prompts diminished consumer loyalty while fulfilled clients spreading positive verbal exchange may make new clients for a business.

Parasuraman et al (1991) distinguished informal, individual needs, past experience, and outside interchanges to affect clients' desires. Mittal and Kamakura (2001) had brought up that conduct aims could conceivably be exact indicator of conduct. In any case, the faithful client regularly "spread the uplifting news" and prescribe the administrations to a few others (Anderson and Sullivan 1990; Reiched and Sasser 1990; Zeithaml et. al. 1996). Banwett and Dasta (1999) perceived that administration and clients fulfillment were basic for holding present clients and drawing in new ones. Maintenance of present clients was needy upon the fulfillment with the present administration. Zeithaml et al (1996) opined that conduct result could be caught by repurchase goal, informal, devotion, grumbling conduct and value affectability. Higher administration quality regularly prompts good conduct result while a lower administration quality prompts horrible social results.

Burston et al (2003) inferred that clients experience was identified with social results. The more constructive the clients experience, the more probable the individual in question was happy to reuse the administration and furthermore indicated that mental variables that impacted customers' conduct included inspiration, recognition, learning, disposition, character, self idea, social class and reference gathering. Khan (2001) expressed that the family was the most significant of the essential gathering and was the most grounded wellspring of impact on buyer conduct. The family convention and traditions were found out by kids and they soaked up numerous standards of conduct from their relatives both deliberately and unwittingly. The examination likewise expressed that the brand name of the retail outlet had an insignificiant impact on the clients' impression of value while acquiring TVs. For example Consumers might want to purchase shading TV from rumored outlet they alloted greatest significance to its vicinity as opposed to its picture.

Fornell et al (1996) found a negative relationship between's consumer loyalty scores and client grumblings. As it were, higher consumer loyalty levels lead to a diminished number of client objections while in the meantime improving client dependability (Fornell and Wernerfeldt 1987; Johnson et. al. 2001). In the event that an organization can decrease the occurrence of client objections effectively, it will improve client dependability (Fornell 1992; Tax et. al. 1998). Grievance, criticism from clients can likewise be utilized for the advancement and improvement of items and administrations (Hart et. al. 1990; Slater and Narver 1995; Soderlund 1998).

Homburg et al (2006) think about was that fulfillment was the essential ward variable, and as the relationship between buyer resolve (CS), association quality (SQ), and verbal focuses (WoM) was all around point by point (Teas 1993; Parasuraman et al 1994b; Spreng et al 1996; Caruana 1999; Spreng and Shi 2005), this article extends suffering organization by looking effect of a degree of feelings on CS, SQ, and WoM destinations at various stages during an all-inclusive administration experience. Disappointed clients, regardless of whether individual or business, really whine about the item or administration (Plymire 1991; Barlow and Moller 1996; Soderlund 1998; Goodman and Newman 2003; George et. al. 2007). Naumann and Giel (1995) expressed that the most widely recognized explanation behind clients not to explain their objections is that it raises a lot of ruckus. This presumably included a cost/advantage tradeoff between the likelihood of getting some potential advantage against the time and exertion important to really gripe. Another related reason was that the client may feel that grumbling would not do any great; and that the provider would simply overlook the protest. A few clients may fear a future response in administration conveyance on the off chance that they grumble. Others may not realize where to really record a protest. It had been assessed that 30 – 60 % of client objections go unsaid, contingent on the idea of the result of administration (TARP 1986).

Chebat et al (2005) found that the inability to grumble was identified with the "Looking for Redress Propensity" idea. This idea implies that clients know from their own experience what adapting conduct they were probably going to take and what results were probably going to result from that conduct. Subsequently, ensuring purchaser fulfillment was considered as crucial to an association's piece of the overall industry and gainfulness (Anderson et. al. 1994) and (Oliver 1997). In view of the past investigations, fulfillment or disappointment of the clients impacts the conduct result either positive or negative way.

Characterization OF SERVICES

The remarkable idea of the administrations and qualities has made various specialists to present different administration order conspires in the current writing (Nelson 1970; Dabry and Karni 1973; Mills and Margulies 1980 and Lovelock 1983). The properties of administrations that incorporate pursuit, experience and assurance characteristics, will impact the results of purchaser's basic leadership (Nelson 1970; Darby and Karni 1973; Mitra and Capella 1997). Nelson (1970) utilize search and familiarity distinctiveness to recognize items and administration. Search character are traits that can be assess before a buy (Mitra and Capella 1997; Mattila 1999; Mitra Reiss and Capella 1999; Mattila and Wirtz 2002).

Numerous fabric retail are solid in pursuit characteristics; in this way buyers can without much of a stretch assess the characteristics of these products before manufacture any buys (Mattila and Wirtz 2002). Experience individuality are persons properties that can be assess simply after the management has been convey or expended (Mitra and Capella 1997; Mitra et al 1999; Pires and Stanton 2000; Hansen 2005). The vast preponderance of the administration display occurrence characteristics on explanation of the five attributes of administration, which are, immaterialness; perishability; indivisibility; heterogeneity and nonattendance of proprietorship (Bennett et .al. 2003 and DeShields et. al. 2005).

Therefore, purchasers would need to encounter the administrations before they can survey the administrations. Darby and Karni (1973) have long-drawn-out the Nelson's system by amalgamation assurance individuality as a characteristic of the character of administrations. Belief individuality are characterize as "administration properties that can't be assessed by purchasers with any sureness even after they have encountered the administration procedure" (Bennett et. al. 2003). The vast majority of the expert administrations display confidence characteristics in light of the fact that the buyers don't have the capacities to impartially assess the average of the administration performed (Bennett et al. 2003). Administrations which are towering in confidence characteristics present larger amounts of apparent hazard (Ostrom and Iacobucci 1995). Thusly, individual impact and informal exposure assume significant jobs in affecting shopper's choice procedure in encountering proficient administrations (Perry and Hamm 1969). Items/Services with high hunt characteristics furnish more data and items with high belief characteristics give less item data to customers in the obtaining basic leadership process (Mitra et. al. 1999). Buyers might be far fetched about the belief guarantees as these cases can't be evaluated and demonstrated even after they have been bought or expended.

Administrations MARKETING AND HIGHER EDUCATION

Advanced teaching division is selected in the test as it has the character of an management industry, for example, immaterialness, perishability, connection, heterogeneity and absence of possession (Hill 1995; Shank et. al. 1995; Lovelock 2001).

Advanced education is like that of the other expert administrations, displaying and having confidence characteristics on the grounds that the understudies don't have the capacities to equitably assess the standard of the administrations performed (Bennett et. al. 2003). It additionally meets the criteria of administrations promoting and consequently ought to be a piece of administrations showcasing (Mazzarol 1998).

As per Mazzarol (1998), "

(1) Education as an administration is coordinated to the general population. Understudies' cooperation in the learning formula can be critical to progress;

(2) Education includes a long-drawn-out and official relationship education grows, one must have increasing concern about the maintenance and assurance of quality. The term quality needs to be well defined for education sector. Quality is about fulfilling and delivering the promise made by the institutions and also meeting the expectations of the stakeholders.

The value of management educational institutions as a source of knowledge production has been challenged. The research output has increased but it lacks relevance and practical impact in the business world. At the same time the economic viability of management educational institution is uncertain. This provokes the thought of few aspect regarding the success strategies and direction of management educational institutions in future.

DISCONFIRMATION OF EXPECTATIONS THEORY

The middle thought of association quality is the disconfirmation of needs conjecture (Dawes and Rowley 1999). Disconfirmation will be mold in view of captivating a gander at the wants and idea of the organization used (Ruyter et al 1997) and thusly the result of the disconfirmation impact the clear association quality (Gotlieb et. al. 1994; Philip and Hazlett 1997). Customers will be content if the association movement waterfall into the extent of region of opposition (Parasuraman 2004). Zone of suppleness is portray as "how much clientele see and are glad to be familiar with" the assortment of the association implementation (Zeithaml and Bitner 2003). The two sort of disconfirmation are sure disconfirmation and unhelpful disconfirmation. Right when the arrangement of the organization outperforms the previous wants, patrons will shape positive disconfirmation and contentment. While, as prior desires outperform effecting of the organization, customers will form negative disconfirmation and displeasure (Ruyter et. al. 1997). Negative disconfirmation will create the negative crash towards the obvious idea of the organization offered (Gotlieb et. al. 1994).

Despite the way that disconfirmation of wants theory gives a framework to take a gander at wants and impression of the organizations, it misses the mark on the quantitative fundamentals that can be associated usually over the activities (Baggs and Kleiner 1996). In like manner, outperforming wants may be firm to attain and is hard to operationalise in light of the way that there is no budgetary purposes behind giving higher than foreseen quality (Johnston 2004). Thusly, this may be seen by the clients as overpricing of organizations and may therefore, result in terrible presentation (Johnston 2004). In any case, the enduring composition reinforces the association flanked by the disconfirmation of wants hypothesis and the clear association quality observationally (Parasuraman et al. 1988; Brown and Swartz 1989). Thusly, this assessment will get disconfirmation of needs speculation as a chapter to assess the general understudies' obvious organization quality on various institutional quality factors.

Foundation QUALITY FACTORS

A mix of determinants of the general understudies' obvious organization quality got from various examinations give a full view to the managers of the higher educational foundations to grasp the general understudies' evident organization quality subject to the suppositions and analysis from the academicians and understudies. Determinants, for instance, 'contact workforce', 'nature of guardians', 'access to workplaces', 'instructive program', 'physical workplaces', and 'staff responsiveness' were gotten reliant on the 'back to front' approach to manage evaluate understudies' clear organization quality (LeBlanc and Nguyen 1997; Nagata et al 2004; Sohail and Shaikh 2004); determinants, for instance, standing of the foundation plus academic agenda, 'extracurricular behavior, and 'cost of course obtainable were grasped subordinate 'ostensibly in' approach to manage survey understudies' obvious organization quality (Kennington et .al. 1996; Joseph et. al. 2005).

The guidance quality pointers for the advantage data model, as shown by Cheng (2003), may fuse first class understudies, qualified staff, better workplaces and rigging, better staff-understudies extent, and cash related assistance. As shown by McDonnell (1995), the going with eight components are to be seen as when surveying school choice, insightful standing, size of school, physical zone, selectivity of train, cash connected guide ease of use, academic agenda openness, understudy body ample and community condition. Hence, the objective of this investigation is to survey and endorse the general understudies' obvious nature of six foundation quality variables, for instance, zone, scholastics, picture, establishment, cost and work power towards enlightening associations offering the officials program.

Sentiments

Sentiments are incredible components, more surprising in nature than points of view, and with a closer relationship to the updates that succinct them (Batson et al 1992; Bigne and Andreu 2004). Feelings are article created and can last between several minutes seconds and couple of minutes. Specifically, Izard (1991) portrayed inclination as 'a propensity that moves, principle forces, and controls nature, thought, and activity'. Lazarus (1991) fight that feeling requires an examination of the circumstance and its outcomes. Oatley and Jenkins (1996) recommended that learning about looks for a psychological state, causing essential changes, facial and vocal clarifications, and is generally trailed by activities. Assessments are high power flooding with tendency gives; an inescapable consequence of the general open's capacity or slightness to achieve their goals (Lazarus 1991; Oatley and Jenkins 1992). At last, Westbrook and Oliver (1991) proposed utilization assumptions as the philosophy of super hot reactions evoked explicitly during thing use or use encounters (for example fulfillment, trance and dread) or by the essential estimations (for example flawlessness/awfulness, releasing up/development).

Fundamentally, opinions sway relations with the earth, and are key for survival, in light of their versatile properties.

Emotional DISSONANCE

Sweeney et al (2000) confined the form of racket into a mental and an energetic fragment. The scholarly fragment concerns clients' retrospection of the respectability of the choice made, while the enthusiastic part is the psychological uneasiness blended ensuing to the decision. Understudies depicted the preparation quality in enthusiastic and mental route by methods for an evaluation structure (Wei and Yan 2008) during the path toward assessing the idea of guidance in schools and scholastics, and understudies' quality satisfaction.

Understudies' SATISFACTION

Kotler and Clarke (1987) described satisfaction as the typical aftereffect of an endeavor or occupation that fulfills one's respect. Rad and Yarmohammadian (2006) portrayed satisfaction as the stubborn accomplishment which results in a solitary's joy. As demonstrated by Dyson et al (1996), the organization quality is the regulated yield passed on by an organization. The organization quality in the informational division particularly in the higher educational associations is the fundamental piece of enlightening flawlessness. As demonstrated by Alridge and Rowley (2001), when understudies see the establishment's quality and organized learning condition supported with academic staff, legitimate workplaces of learning and structure, their energy for their affiliation would increase and would be appeared positive direct. The understudies are prodded from the academic similarly as the administrative capability of their foundation.

With respect to guidance establishments, satisfaction is the resultant consequence of a foundation's definitive similarly as informational system's keen introduction (Zeithaml 1988). According to Spooreen et al (2007), the progressive congruity, teachers' academic limit, capable headway, straightforwardness in understudies' appraisal, analysis and planning are the huge features that judiciously develop the understudies. Rodie and Kleine (2000) put a view that the understudies would be induced, loyal and extraordinary performers if their establishment holds principal educational workplaces with suitable school staff. The teachers' show in the class and outside the class is an imperative segment of improving understudies' unbiased nature, motivation and satisfaction.

The understudies are fantastically affected by the enlightening activities of their instructor or educator who headings them. Shevlin et al (2000) communicated that understudies are content with the educators who teach with unwavering quality, exactness, reasonableness and keen procedure in an understudy pleasing way. Elliot and Shin (2002) and Dalton and Denson (2009) communicated that understudies measurement of satisfaction increases by working with those course instructors and speakers who properly handle the assignments, exercises, tests and energize understudies' reasonable reasoning and tendency improvement.

The openness of other academic workplaces, for instance, insightful staff, specialists, carrier coordinating division are the features that an establishment necessities for its understudies' better execution and satisfaction (Bolton and Drew 1991). The understudies' satisfaction is seen by the coordinated effort of the legitimate staff and the work force with the understudies. Prevailing piece of the understudies get de-enlivened in case they found that the staff isn't thoughtful and kind.

Attitude

Attitudes are commonly relentless, genuine estimations that make as reiterated positive or negative energetic responses over some stretch of time. As demonstrated by the Theory of Planned Behavior, mood towards the lead is implied the positive or negative feelings an individual has on a particular direct (Ajzen and Fishbein 1980). Attitude towards direct is a part of one's striking feeling about playing out the lead and an evaluation of the outcomes coming about on account of the direct (Chang 1998). As demonstrated by Ghen and Liu (2004), mindset is a basic factor influencing social point.

Particular attitude towards the direct mirrors how much an individual has a positive or negative perspective on the lead. Tempers about direct are managed by individuals, feelings about the consequence of playing out that lead, and each conviction is weighted by the dynamic estimation of the outcome being alluded to (Ajzen 2001; Tan and Laswad

BEHAVIOURAL OUTCOME

Behavioural outcome could be measured based on two factors: Firstly, when customers (students in case of educational institutions) say positive things, recommend the institution, remain loyal, spend more time with the institution and pay premium price. Secondly, when customers say negative things, switch to another institution, complain to others or spend less time with the institution. Behavioural outcome of individual depends on the level of service quality (Zeithaml et. al. 1996). Dynamically prominent purchaser faithfulness will induce positive client direct, for example, rehash buys, positive verbal correspondences, which thusly lead to progressively basic piece of the general business and higher net gain for the association firms (Parasuraman et. al. 1994). As to kind of social result influenced by association quality and fulfillment, verbal exchange is a hero among the most all things considered utilized segments. Parasuramman et al (1991) found that when buyers' impression of association quality are high, buyers are slanted to prescribe the relationship to different people. Besides, Reichhelds and Sasser (1990) displayed that held clients pull in new clients through positive verbal. Moreover, Zeithaml (2000), pushed the possibility that technique with client's may support the affiliations uncommon notoriety to new clients. Different scientists have demonstrated that when clients seen to have encountered more terrible association execution than anticipated they are apparently going to challenge to untouchables (for example negative verbal).

SCHOOL PRACTICES

A school practice is a method or approach that has appeared to dependably incite an ideal f edifying outcome. An assurance to utilizing the practices in planning is an affirmation to utilizing all the learning and headway open to one to guarantee edifying achievement. This term is utilized an extraordinary piece of the time in the fields of school affiliation, the instructive framework, and school movement. The school practice is a well-portrayed strategy that adds to a profitable advancement in illuminating improvement. A touch of the more generally utilized are: an iterative movement process, basic association, quality control, and change control.

(1) An iterative (which means dull) is the improvement framework, which advances in persevering stages, keeps up a highlight on sensible undertakings and guarantees that past stages are gainful before the later stages are attempted.

(2) Requirement the authorities watches out for the issue of crawling basics, which is a condition wherein the customer demands extra movements to what are past the level of what was at first composed. To prepare for this standard supernatural occurrence, need the authorities utilizes structures, for example, documentation of fundamentals, sign-offs, and approachs.

(3) Quality control is a strategy that portrays target measures for examining quality all through the improvement framework to the degree the thing's support, faithful quality, and execution.

(4) Change control is a framework that looks to enthusiastically screen changes all through the iterative method to guarantee that records are impeccable for changes that have been made and that disallowed changes are not tried.

Wikipedia the free Encyclopedia (2011) states that school practice is a methodology or structure that has constantly appeared to be better than those developed with different strategies, and that is utilized as a benchmark. Working practice is a basic association term utilizing to keep up quality as a decision rather than required coordinated models and can be built up on self-appraisal or benchmarking. Best school practice is a part of certification the authorities measures, for example, ISO 9000 and ISO 14001. Recording and spreading out methodology and practices is a captured and dull procedure reliably sidestepped the best techniques constantly. A key limit required when applying practice to affiliations is the capacity to change the uncommon characteristics of an association with the practices that it gives in every way that really matters to other individuals.

From the noteworthiness of ¬practice! also, ¬school practice! Referenced above, it may be mulled over that school practice is a procedure or system utilized by school that has reliably appeared to be unrivaled accomplish as a benchmark. The school practice plans to advance to finish up being better as upgrades utilizing the genuine use of a thought, conviction, or method, rather than speculations identifying with the standard. It is utilized to keep up quality by the as regularly as possible rehashed or standard activity; consistent execution; a development of shows of a comparable kind; use; tendency; custom; day by day timetable concerning making standard sections of records; routine regarding well ordered exercise; and deliberate exercise for course or solicitation improvement. The schools need to contribute a time of imperativeness for executing as regularly as would be prudent, more than once, all things considered, persistently of an improvement or expertise to progress toward getting the opportunity to be capacity. The school practice is considered to depict the way toward making and following a standard technique for doing things that various affiliations can utilize. Thusly, in the school rehearses, the use of hypothetical science or information, measures, rules, structure, way, requesting of driving and continuing with suits and arraignments through their different stages, must be required by the necessities of men and affiliations.

Rigid Quality Management (TQM) related with class

Planning today is piled up with new difficulties because of a constantly extraordinary understudy and teacher masses, mechanical advances and changes in direction content. Despite these issues getting ready must keep up quality crosswise over examination passages schools and affiliation type. Since rigid quality association gives an instrument to help guarantee this quality. The full scale quality association (TQM) can be utilized as a usage of theoretical science or learning, measures, rules, structure, way, requesting of planning and continuing with suits and arraignments through their different stages for the school rehearses.

Dheeraj Mehrotra (2001) recognize that the Deming's idea of TQM gives key convictions to class practice. The likelihood of TQM is relevant to class can be seen as them the "Four Principles of Total Quality Management."

1: Synergistic Relationships:

As exhibited by this standard, a connection must center, to the avoidance of everything else, on its providers and clients. In a TQM association, everybody is both a client and provider; this confounding idea features "the careful idea of the work where all are fused". At the day's end, coordinated effort and encouraged effort are focal. The very utilization of the guideline standard of TQM to direction underlines the synergistic relationship between the "providers" and "clients". The likelihood of pleasant imperativeness prescribes that presentation and age is refreshed by pooling the limit and experience of people.

In an examination anteroom, teacher understudy get-togethers are what could be diverged from industry's cutting edge specialists. The result of their profitable work together is the movement of the understudy's abilities, interests, and character. In one sense, the understudy is the educator's client, as the beneficiary of enlightening affiliations fit the understudy's advancement and improvement. Found thusly, the educator and the school are providers of functional learning contraptions, conditions, and structures to the understudy, who is the school's central client. The school is responsible for obliging the entire arrangement enlightening welfare of understudies by revealing to them the most ideal approach to learn and give in top notch ways, how to get to quality in their own work and in that of others, and how to put resources into their very own stand-out significant set up and life-wide learning techniques by expanding open doors for headway in each bit of reliably life. In another sense, the understudy is in like way a laborer, whose thing is essentially his or her own one of a kind reliable improvement and self-improvement.

2: Continuous Improvement and Self Evaluation

The second standard of TQM related with instructing is the firm force to solid improvement, eye to eye and all around. Inside a Total normal quality school setting, chief work pleasantly with their supporters: educators. Rigid monstrosity is, along these lines, a triumph win approach which attempts propelling everybody's certain potential bit of leeway. As appeared by Deming, no individual being ought to ever regard another person being. In this manner, TQM supplement self examination as a component of an unending improvement practice. In addition, this code besides overlays to the thought on understudies' quality, particular information styles, and exceptional sorts of bits of learning.

3: A System of Ongoing Process

The third code of TQM as related in quick is the perceive of the relationship as a framework and the work done inside the association must be viewed as a strategy with technique. The essential consequences of this code is that individual understudies and teacher are less to blame for stoppage than the relationship in which they work. Quality area operational on the structure, which should be look at to perceive and discard the defective approach that enable its part to come up short. Since structure are included technique, the improvement made in the faultlessness of those strategy, everything considered, pick the transcendence of the subsequent thing. In the new model of learning, dreary improvement of information frameworks dependent on smarts results supplant the obsolete "train and test" mode.

So as to accomplish the above as chance to the school condition, in adding to determination, participatory running among pleasing and well-informed associates is crucial to the success of TQM in schooling; everyone mixed up must comprehend and believe in principles. Some recruits who are unswerving to the ethics can aid success with TQM. Their visualization and skills in control, management, interpersonal message, problem solving and original collaboration are significant qualities for winning completion of TQM.

Chizmar (2001) indicate that TQM in school practice i.e. the knowledge and education process implies a joint and far reaching satisfaction of considerations got from the social gathering TQM model. In this establishment, TQM is, subsequently, a point of view that spotlights see on the running farthest achieves that change learning. Steyn (2000) reinforces Chizmar4s explanation and depicts TQM as focus on achieve quality. TQM can be explicit as a point of view and a gigantic measure of controlling credits that intend to get together and beat perspective of various outside and inward client base. The consequent heart is on the creation and mission for enthusiastic walk around as the basic noteworthy set or target of achieve quality through sharing of occupation players in a school. Morgan, C., and Murgatroyd, S. (1997) insinuate this as the profitable directing of an affiliation customer supplier relatives in order to guarantee affordable, sheer grade headway in quality acquaintance and pass on with the five arrangement of affiliation and organization explicitly: message, ensure, culture, vision, and reinforcing.

Kathleen Cotton (2001) rational Deming fourteen point for brightness in train as the seek after:

(1) Create and proceed with a consistent quality of limit toward improvement of understudies and organization. Plan to make the best quality analyst fit for enlightening a wide range of system and entering essential positions in human headway. Enlightening affiliation must mix to the test, need to get acquainted with their standard occupations, and take on the board for alter.

(2) Work to put an end to assessing and the destructive effects of score people. Focus on the adjusting course, not the rating course.

(3) Cease reliance on testing to achieve quality. Crash the require for audit on a mass foundation (organized achievement tests) by to the extent that learning foundation which make quality presentation; learning information that give sureness imagination and experimentation.

(4) Work with the instructional establishments from which understudy come. Point of confinement entire cost of edification by enlightening the relationship by strategies for follower sources and decision to propel the idea of understudy pending into your system.

(5) Improve reliably and everlastingly the strategy of understudy redesiging and organization to recover quality and yield in up close and personal life and the overall public.

(6) Institute determined planning at work for understudy, teacher, secret staff and administrator; for all people associated with the human connection or social event of people.

(7) Institute the board. The purpose of the board (specialist) ought to be to enable people to utilize learning and advantages for complete an improved movement and set the speed lashing human cleverness.

(8) Drive out dread with the objective that everybody may work gainfully for the school plot. Make a surroundings which urge people to speak liberally and take risks.

(9) Break downward barriers between department. People in education, special education, secretarial, food service, management, curriculum growth and research have to work as a team. Develop strategy for growing the collaboration among groups and human being people. Planning moment in time will facilitate this go-ahead.

(10) Eliminate slogan, exhortations, and target for teachers and student asking for perfect show and new dimensions of yield. Urgings make ill-disposed undertakings. The greater part of the reasons for low greatness and low yield have a place with the plan and therefore lie far off the control of teacher and student.

Institute leadership (modern methods of supervision)

The aims of management (leadership) should help the train members use skill and resources to do better job plus set the pace driving person creativity. The school be supposed to bring one and all to emphasis the aim of learning for all. It resources removing attainment gaps for all inhabitants groups for a group toward excellence and equity. Emphasis have to be on the excellence of the total programme rather than person behaviours. New relationships between administrator and teacher and teachers and student must be created and maintain. Leadership roles of administrator can help teachers and student do the best job potential

Institute a vigorous programme of education and self-improvement.

A broad understanding of the past, the facility to assess the measures that led to the present, and the talent to forecast past needs are indispensable. Employees be required to be repeatedly acquiring new information, skills, and method. The school head and school member have to be retrained in new method of school based organization, checking pack components, getting structure, and joint styles of basic leadership. All accomplices on the school's side must comprehend that improvement in understudy satisfaction will make bigger measure of issue, not less hazard.

Execution of Total Quality Management (TQM)

Notwithstanding the way that the TQM thought is sound, execution accomplishment is changed depending on the techniques associated with to achieve the affiliation targets of significant worth faultlessness. A couple TQM approach are portrayed as seek after:

Crumrine and Runnels (1991) offer a model for executing TQM in a school that perceives five phases or classes:

(1) Commitment. Look at, evaluate, get, and secure obligation to TQM.

(2) Organizational Development. Fuse TQM into key organization shapes; educate, train, and offer assistance to agents.

(3) Customer Focus. Choose work gatherings; dismember customers, things/organizations.

(4) Process Orientation. Perceive, standardize, and improve technique control.

(5) Continuous Improvement. Make strategy for recognizing openings and organizing the improvement method into step by step undertakings.

Joseph Jablonski (1992)well-known three self necessary for achievement of TQM to succeed inside an organization: participative organization; incessant process improvement; and the use of teams.

• Participative organization refers to the close involvement of all member of a company in the organization process, thus deemphasizing conventional top-down organization method. In other words, manager set policy and make key decision only with the input and supervision of the subordinate who will have to execute and adhere to the orders. This technique improve upper management's grasp of operation and, more prominently, is an main motivator for people who begin to feel as if they enclose control and ownership of the procedure in which they contribute.

- **Preparation**

During training, management decide whether or not to follow a TQM program. They undergo first training, recognize needs for outside consultant, develop a exact vision and goals, draft a company policy, entrust the necessary capital, and converse the goals all through the organization.

- **Planning**

In the preparation stage, a full plan of completion is drafted (including budget and schedule), the communications that will bear the program is reputable, and the resources necessary to start the plan are earmark and secured.

- **Assessment**

This stage emphasize a methodical self-assessments with input as of clientele/clients of the character and individuality of individuals in the corporation, as well as the corporation as a whole.

- **Implementation**

At this point, the club can already begin to settle on its return on its asset in TQM. It is during this segment that support human resources are chosen and taught, and managers and the workers are trained. Training entail raising workers' unconsciousness of exactly what TQM involve and how it can help them and the corporation. It also explains each worker's role in the agenda and explains what is predictable of all the personnel.

• **Diversification**

In this stage, manager utilize their TQM experience and successes to bring group outside the society (suppliers, distributors, and other company that have an blow on the business's overall health) into the value process. Diversification behavior include instruction, rewarding, underneath, and partner with groups that are embrace by the organization TQM initiatives.

Ho S.K., Wearn K. (1996) Total eminence running resulted in major reestablishes in steady quality and students4 satisfaction. The focal degrees of TQM are relied upon to achieve creative ensured improvement through the help and commitment of school staff all through a school. TQM considers the upsides of a relationship in the wake of get-together the necessities of customers (both inside and outside), using clear contraptions and structures to check results and help key pro.

Jadvyga Ramanauskiene and Julius Ramanauskas (2006) valued the models of Total Quality Management in getting ready and intrigue plots. Quality interest structure is routinely related for the whole improvement concerning the likelihood of thing and affiliation. Normal occasions of the sales of gigantic worth the specialists system are as demonstrated by the going with:

Stage 1.

Framework work for the improvement of titanic worth the board structure:

• Decision to make quality association structure (the contemplations of the pioneer of the affiliation)

- The methodology of the standard program
- The examination of TQM benchmarks and TQM theory
- Formation of obvious and work packs for the introduction of TQM process
- The examination of the present bits of epic worth structure
- The technique of the program for quality structure creation
- Preparation of epic worth way of thinking
- Distribution of motivations driving control and supports as showed up by the bits of huge worth structure

Stage 2.

The straightforwardness and execution of the records of the quality association structure:
- Documentation structure and piece
- Working out the timetable for report sorting out
- Document overseeing and execution

Stage 3.

The sorting out of the quality connection structure for accreditation: The examination of the quality affiliation system (inside mind blowing study with the help of administrators)
- Correcting practices and their accreditation
- The choice of a declaration establishment, reports arranging • Presentation of the procedures for an accreditation foundation
- Creation of clarification conditions

usiness Excellence (2011) proposes the use of full scale quality association (TQM) as voyage for after:
- Train top relationship on TQM measures.

- Assess the current: Culture, purchaser suffering quality, and quality getting structure.
- Top union picks the key examinations and checks and passes on them. •Develop a TQM end-all structure
- Identify and sort out customer needs and pick things or relationship to address those issues.
- Determine the key structures that produce those things or affiliations.
- Create process improvement social gatherings.
- Managers vitalize the undertakings by coordinating, building, and offering central fixations for the social gathering. • Management headings changes for movement in unendingly structure the specialists. After updates systematization occurs.
- Evaluate advance against plan and change as required.
- Provide clear ace idea and information. Set up a pro change/check process.

CHAPTER 3

Underutilized Learning Techniques

The expectation of this guide is to assist you with being a more viable student in time administration, note-taking, perusing, and planning for exams. Amid your first year at college, specifically, you might discover what sort of student you are. It may be vital for you to investigate and try different things with various methods for learning and working with material to perceive what works for you. Indeed, you may find that you utilize distinctive learning methodologies for various study's to process scholarly data with the goal that you comprehend and recall it. Everybody has an alternate method for learning and there's nobody right route for everybody or for eadid not update it. Shouldn't they quit utilizing these strategies and start utilizing ones that are historic? Clinicians have be making and look over the responsiveness of system for study and headline for over 100 years. In any casing, several persuading procedures are underutilizedch study you're contemplating. In any case, the urgent component is that you're effectively occupied with the procedure by contemplating data from different edges as opposed to exclusively the manner in which it's been displayed in addresses. This methodology will set you up well to be a basic scholar and for getting ready adequately for assignments, tests and exams.

The more methodologies you convey to contemplate, the better will be your understanding, maintenance and review. This Guide acquaints a progression of procedures with assist you with fostering profound realizing which requires dynamic commitment with the material, while surface learning is the place you have just a shallow comprehension of the data, and experience issues disclosing and applying it to different ideas or settings. By taking part in a profound methodology not exclusively will your learning be more compelling yet there's a more prominent probability that you'll upgrade your learning background and happiness at college. Keep in mind that dynamic commitment is foremost to viable learning.

In the event that straightforward methods were accessible that educators and understudies could use to enhance understudy learning and accomplishment, be astounded if instructors were not being told about these procedures and if numerous understudies were not utilizing them? Imagine a scenario where understudies were rather receiving inadequate learning strategies that undermined their accomplishment, or if nothing else did not develop it. Shouldn't they quit utilize these methods and set up utilize ones that are powerful? Clinicians have be creating and assess the viability of system for study and leadership for over 100 existence. In any case, a number of forceful events are underutilized—numerous educators don't find out about them, and thus numerous understudies don't utilize them, in spite of proof proposing that the methods could profit understudy accomplishment with little included exertion. Likewise, some learning methods that are well known and regularly utilized by understudies are generally incapable. One potential explanation behind the distinction between investigate on the adequacy of learning strategies and their utilization in instructive practice is that on the grounds that such huge numbers of procedures are accessible, it would challenge for teachers to filter through the critical research to pick which ones show affirmation of reasonableness and could in every practical sense be acknowledged by understudies (Pressley, Goodchild, Fleet, Zajchowski, and Evans, 1989).

Toward surveillance out for this bother, we investigated the sufficiency of 10 learning frameworks that understudies possibly will use to recover their blooming over a wide gathering of matter domains.1 The knowledge procedure we think here be picked dependent on the accompanying criteria. We picked a few strategies (e.g., self-testing, circulated rehearse) in light of the fact that an underlying overview of the writing showed that they could enhance understudy accomplishment over an extensive variety of conditions. Different systems (e.g., rehashing and featuring) were incorporated in light of the fact that understudies report utilizing them as often as possible. Additionally, understudies are in charge of controlling an expanding measure of their taking in as they advance from basic evaluations through center school and secondary school to school. Deep rooted students likewise need to keep directing their very own realizing, regardless of whether it happens with regards to postgraduate training, the work environment, the improvement of new leisure activities, or recreational exercises. Along these lines, we constrained our decisions to methods that might be actualized by understudies devoid of assist (e.g., without require trend setting novelty or broad materials that would require to be set up by an educator). Some grounding might be required for understudies to figure out how to utilize a method with constancy, however on a fundamental level, understudies ought to have the capacity to utilize the systems without supervision. We additionally picked systems for which an adequate measure of observational proof was accessible to help somewhere around a starter evaluation of potential viability. Obviously, we couldn't survey every one of the trial that meet these condition, given the inside and out natural history of our review, and these criteria avoided a few systems that show much guarantee, for example, methods that are driven by cutting edge innovations.

Since instructors are destined to find out about these methods in instructive brain science classes, we analyzed how some instructive brain research course readings affirmed them (Ormrod, 2008; Santrock, 2008; Slavin, 2009; Snowman, McCown, and Biehler, 2009; Sternberg and Williams, 2010; Woolfolk, 2007). Disregarding the confirmation of a bit of the frameworks, countless this looking into material did not give satisfactory idea, which would join dynamic reviews of their sensibility and examinations of their generalizability and potential tangles. As necessities be, for most by far of the learning procedure recorded in Table 1, we considered the creation to confine the generalizability of their central thinks transversely different classes of parts—materials, learning conditions, understudy characteristics, and reason endeavors. The choice of these classes was blended by Jenkins' (1979) depict (for an event of its utilization in illuminating settings, see Marsh and Butler, in press), and models of each depiction are seemed, by all accounts, to be Table 2. Materials identify with the specific substance that understudies are depended upon to learn, study, or handle. Learning conditions identify with parts of the setting in which understudies are interfacing with the to-be told materials. These conditions join bits of the learning condition itself (e.g., tumult versus quietness in a homeroom), yet they, metaphorically, identify with the way by which a learning structure is understands it. For instance, a system could be used just once or all things considered (a variable suggested as estimation) when understudies are asking about, or a structure could be used when understudies are either analyzing or hoping to-be told materials. Any number of understudy properties could about impact the sensibility of a given learning structure. For example, in contrast with further developed understudies, more youthful understudies in early evaluations may not profit by a method. Understudies' essential psychological capacities, for example, working memory limit or general liquid insight, may likewise impact the viability of a given strategy. In an instructive setting, space information alludes to the substantial, pertinent learning an understudy conveys to an exercise.

Understudies with some area learning about a point may likewise think that its less demanding to utilize self-clarification and elaborative cross examination, which are two procedures that include replying "why" inquiries regarding a specific idea (e.g., "For what reason would particles of ice ascend inside a cloud?"). Area information may get better the recompense of rickety and featuring also. By the by, albeit some space information will profit understudies as they start adapting new substance inside a given area, it's anything but an essential for utilizing the greater part of the learning systems. How much the viability of each learning procedure gets crosswise over long maintenance interims and sums up crosswise over various paradigm undertakings is of basic significance.

In talking about how the strategies impact standard execution, we underscore examinations that have gone history exhibiting enhanced recollection for aim material by estimating understudies' cognizance, application, and exchange of learning. Note, in any case, that in spite of the fact that increasing genuine learning isn't viewed as the main or extreme goal of tutoring, we audaciously consider endeavors to enhance understudy maintenance of information as fundamental for achieving other instructional destinations; in the event that one doesn't recollect center thoughts, certainties, or ideas, applying them may demonstrate troublesome, if certainly feasible. Understudies who have overlooked standards of variable based math will be not able apply them to take care of issues or utilize them as an establishment for learning analytics (or material science, financial aspects, or other related spaces), and understudies who don't recollect what operant molding is will probably experience issues applying it to tackle conduct issues. We are not pushing that understudies invest their energy mechanically remembering actualities; rather, we are recognizing the imperative transaction between reminiscence for an idea on one give and the capacity to appreciate and be relevant it on the other.

A point of this monograph is to urge understudies to use the most ideal knowledge method (or structures) to attain a given instructional target. Some knowledge philosophy are usually spun around strengthening understudies' memory for substances (e.g., the watchword mental right hand), others depend more on civilizing approval (e.g., self-clarification), yet next others may revive both reminiscence and cognizance (e.g., tackle testing).

3.1 TIME MANAGEMENT

Supporting any viable investigation system is time administration, an ability that can be educated. Understudies once in a while have a bunch of assignments or tests amid specific times of the semester so it's basic to be composed. Being means to the point that will probably be a successful student, you'll make the most of your chance at college more, and your feelings of anxiety will be limited. The sooner you furnish yourself with great time administration methodologies, the more successful you'll be with your investigation on the grounds that having an arrangement centers your psyche. Keep in mind that companions, relaxation and game are critical for a solid life and that a harmony among work and different exercises will assist you with staying inspired. Great time administration abilities are additionally a benefit in your own life and in your future calling.

On the off chance that you discover one theme or study harder than others, at that point clearly you'll have to dedicate additional opportunity to it. Make sure to consider how much learning occurs in class, labs and instructional exercises versus how much function you're relied upon to do independent from anyone else. It's likewise imperative to know the learning destinations for every one of your studys and the points inside them to guide and structure your investigation and the measure of time you spend on it. Consistently at college is diverse as far as outstanding burden, so you have to adopt an adaptable strategy to oblige changing needs or conditions. A period plan is a guide just, so don't freeze if there are interruptions to it half a month.

3.2 LEARNING TECHNIQUES

We think about the accessible proof for the adequacy of every one of the learning strategies. Each audit starts with a concise portrayal of the strategy and a talk regarding why it is relied upon to enhance understudy learning. We at that point think about generalizability (concerning learning conditions, materials, understudy attributes, and rule assignments), feature any examination on the system that has been directed in agent instructive settings, and address any distinguished issues for executing the strategy. In like manner, the surveys are generally secluded: Each of the 10 audits is sorted out around these subjects (with relating headers) so perusers can undoubtedly recognize the most important data without fundamentally perusing the monograph completely

Toward the finish of each audit, we give a general appraisal to every system as far as its moderately utility—low, direct, or far above the ground. Understudies plus educator who are not start at now responsibility everything considered ought to consider utilizing procedures doled out as high utility, in light of the manner in which that the impacts of these systems are strong and entire up widely. Structures could have be assign as low utility or straight utility for any figure of reasons. For example, a scheme could have1 been doled out as low usefulness since its possessions are obliged to a little division of resources that understudies need to obtain in; the organization might be significant occasionally and gotten a handle on in fitting settings, meanwhile, with respect to trade strategies, it would be view as low in utility as a effect of its restricted genus lizability. A line of attack could in like way get a low-or direct utility rating on the off chance that it demonstrated guarantee, yet inadequate with regards to affirmation was available to help trust in doling out a higher usefulness assessment. In such luggage, we urge specialist to also seem at these systems inside enlightening settings, in any case understudies and teachers may need to utilize alert before getting a handle on them broadly. Most fundamental, given that every utility evaluation could have been transferred for a game plan of reasons, we talk about the purpose behind a given examination toward the finish of each.

At last, our plan was to lead serious outlines of the part on each knowledge system. For technique that have been review extensively (e.g.,disseminated rehearse), however, we depended on past audit and enhanced them with any examination that show up after they had been spread. For a large figure of the knowledge strategies, an excessive number of articles have been distributed to refer to them all; in this manner, in our exchange of the vast majority of the procedures, we refer to a subset of applicable articles.

DEFINING GOALS

Recognizing objectives are especially essential to maintain a strategic distance from tarrying and help you to stay engaged and propelled. Be clear about what you need to accomplish at college and work out some transient, medium-term and long haul objectives. Ensure that these objectives are sensible and achievable in light of the fact that doing as such means will probably accomplish them. You might be vague about which calling you're going for however you clearly need to pass your exams.

SETTING PRIORITIES

Know your needs for the semester, for the week and for the day. This information will assist you with having an unmistakable thought of what assignments should be accomplished. In any case, having such a large number of high needs could have negative outcomes. Going to addresses, instructional exercises, and labs and meeting task due dates are top needs, yet balance these duties by setting aside a few minutes for social and relaxation.

MAKING ARRANGEMENTS

Making arrangements for the semester, the week and the day includes knowing precisely what undertakings are coming up and making the strides required to accomplish them. A divider organizer, a week by week organizer and a journal are fundamental for you to design fittingly.

SEMESTER PLAN

Have a composed arrangement which factors in dates for assignments and tests for the entire semester. Doing as such means there are no terrible amazements with respect to evaluations and you can see the "lie of the land" for the semester, including periods that might be especially bustling a direct result of a bunch of appraisals or tests.

- This arrangement ought to incorporate dates for assignments, tests, oral introductions, and lab reports.
- Be particular about the data you incorporate into your chance arrangement—e.g. HIST 105 Essay 20% — with the goal that you know the weightings and you can organize errands and plan as needs be.
- Use distinctive shaded pens for various subjects to make following your assignments less demanding.
- Mark in task due dates and work out the time you'll have to finish every one.
- Ask yourself what steps you have to take to plan for them. For instance, if a Essay is expected in three weeks, choose around to what extent you'll spend on look into, arranging, composing, and altering.

- Note these assignments and dates for finishing them in your journal or on a divider organizer. Utilize the estimation of the task (e.g. 15%, 30%) as a manual for to what extent you ought to spend on it.
- Put the arrangement in a noticeable place, for example, in the front of your envelope or journal or on your room divider. That route there are no reasons for not comprehending what your remaining burden is, and there's the fulfillment of having the capacity to tick off undertakings as you finish them.

Try not to limit the significance of taking note of these subtle elements regardless of whether, for instance, a lab report is expected each fortnight and just worth 5%. Staying on track (inside multi day or two) will make the procedure more reasonable, and you'll do more prominent equity to the evaluation. Composing assignments is a procedure which requires some serious energy and reflection, and it can't be rushed. Likewise take note of any work and social duties with the goal that you can unmistakably observe what time you have accessible to finish ponder assignments.

Week after week PLAN

- Work out your needs for the week as far as pending assignments, tests, labs and instructional exercises.
- Don't limit the significance of including openings for doing alloted readings for addresses or instructional exercises as these are critical assignments that additionally compete for your chance.

you'll have the fulfillment of accomplishing the incremental undertakings, and consequently you'll be more disposed to remain inspired. A comparable technique applies to getting ready for a test or exam: what ideas, terms, or hypotheses do you have to return to? Do you discover a few thoughts more troublesome than others? For roughly to what extent do you envision considering each segment with the goal that you traverse all the material before the test or exam? These are essential inquiries to consider so your investigation is deliberate and errands are accomplished on time.

Every day PLAN

Choose your needs for the day and show them in your journal arranged by significance. Arranging every day along these lines will assist you with staying concentrated on the undertakings you need to accomplish.

THE EFFECTIVENESS OF ACTIVE AND PASSIVE TEACHING METHODS

Informational and exchange school master recommend that using asking structures acclimated to understudy tendencies and necessities can help understudies not solely to create upkeep of subject altering yet in spite of improve their qualitys, test scores, and higher intrigue aptitudes (Piercy et al., 2012). In any case, all around used appearing, from understudies' perspective, are commonly observed as insufficient incomprehensible and unfit to respond to their necessities for progressively instinctual appearing and appearing with higher component on the real idea of learning (Pietrzykowski and Szczyt, 2012). Similarly, on account of different changes in the open field, business getting ready has been attempted to make a heading framework that is stunningly progressively all around that truly matters arranged (Škudienē, 2012). A structure that would plan understies to work in guaranteed world (Mocinic, 2012), yet likewise associate with them to grow great collaboration capacities, relational and initiative abilities, and in addition critical thinking and expository aptitudes (Mohammad, 2015), is these days alluring.

With a specific end goal to react to these changing requests of the two understudies and society, there was a move in encouraging substance and materials, and additionally in training techniques utilized. Writing survey recommends a move from conventional, instructor focused way to deal with present day, understudy focused methodology. Conventional, more aloof showing strategies (e.g., addresses, works out) situated educators in the focal point of the learning system and empowered transmission of data from instructor to understudies, with understudies being dormant experts of data (e.g., Dowling, Godfrey and Gyles, 2003). Mastermind instructing is considered effi cient for learning exchange, and information procuring is evidently better through oral areas (e.g., Peroz, Beuche and Peroz, 2009). In any case, it isn't effi cient enough for progressively huge energy about the subject, essential thinking, innovative work and comparative (Mocinic, 2012).

Current, more dynamic methodology stresses understudy inclusion and dynamic investment through exchanges and additionally synergistic exercises (Carpenter, 2006). This methodology esteems teachers as co-students, and has a higher spotlight on training than guidance (Škudienē, 2012). Educators go up against another job, the one of a coordinator and organizer of the instructive procedure (Yakovleva and Yakovlev, 2014).

Understudies have the chance to address, talk about and investigate, and gain information as well as build up their aptitudes and dispositions (e.g., Arasti, Falavarjani and Imanipour, 2012).

The efficacy of dynamic encouraging procedures contrasted with customary ones. Applying dynamic showing strategies in a conventional address based course has shown to roll out quantifiable improvements in understudy learning (e.g., de Caprariis, Barman and Magee, 2001; Perkins and Saris, 2001). The joining of dynamic orchestrating structures was appeared to impact signifi can't updates like understudies' edifying execution (e.g., Berg et al., 1995; Dowling, Godfrey and Gyles, 2003; Johnson and Mighten, 2005; Yoder and Hochevar, 2005), and regardless of improve sensible results in class-specifi c materials (e.g., Cui, 2013; Michel, Cater and Varela, 2009). An entire game-plan upkeep of materials appeared in classes has what's more been related with dynamic showing up (van Eynde and Spencer, 1988). Terenzini et al. (2001) address that other than giving progressively clear gains in understudy learning, dynamic structures besides short interminably significant gains in understudies' system, correspondence and get-together aptitudes, while Miller (2004) showed that they brief legitimately important understudy capacity to manage issues and make game approaches. Results in addition show that dynamic frameworks improve learning execution (e.g., Kerr, Troth and Pickering, 2003; Young, Klemz and Murphy, 2003) as understudies consider their immense quality to improve the learning system. In addition, the results revealed that understudies see their creation feeling of how to be intelligently key to their future occupations if dynamic structures are related (Wingfi eld and Black, 2005).

INSTRUMENT

A diagram on the practicality of preparing strategy that are regularly utilized amidst the engaging framework was delivered utilizing things identified in the huge game-plan, and wide and intense individual teaching establishment. Understudies surveyed the reachability of an aggregate of 52 express showing up (TM) that could be affiliated to six get-togethers – looking out for, workshops, single work outside the examination way, store up work outside the examination antechamber, discontinuous TM, and getting learning/aptitudes through data development. They gave their statements on a Likert-type scale from 1 (enabling framework does not add to checking new learning/aptitudes in any capacity by any means) to 4 (masterminding procedure contributes shockingly to expanding new information/limits). Furthermore, the review accumulated respondents' eight estimation properties – sexual bearing, understudy GPA, graduate GPA to date, selection in an understudy affiliation, coordinated effort in an understudy dispute, understudy trade understanding, closeness of any work thought, work duty in the field of stud-ies (suitable work understanding), and volunteering data. The review was pilot endeavored a dash of get-together of understudies.

CHAPTER 4
The Landscape of Indian B-Schools: A Historical Overview

India undeniably has around 1300 and more trade colleges (B-schools) understood by All India Council for Technical Education (AICTE), the pinnacle bolster ace, under Ministry of Human Resources, standard of India, as the connection preparing advancement is nearing its fifth decade. The essential Indian relationship of Management (IIM) was set up at Ahmedabad in 1961. For quite a while huge business colleges in India have been all around thought out into the IIMs and the rest. The IIMs have heading of certainty kept up their best rankings at any rate there are undeniable B-schools who are narrowing the lead. Notwithstanding the manner by which that an association like, IIM-An obviously gives a benchmark, there is close by no capacity between the other B-schools at the best 25 (Sinha 2007).

In the start of the year 2007, while adequate character blowing schools have advancing new plans, the nature of driving bit of foundations still lies far underneath than the scanned for after estimation. At the most key level, in an extremely conventional way, auxiliary inadequacies like training foundation, careless benchmarks, nonattendance of strict standards and so forth make lion's share of these 1300 administration establishments defenseless against evolving times. This is additionally in light of the fact that desires are expanding complex with more unfurling chances of administration training around the world.

the quality parts of administration instruction in India and investigates the conceivable outcomes of getting magnificence in Indian B-schools. the accreditation procedure, both national and comprehensive along with how it can make a payment in accomplish luminosity in business colleges.

4.1 INDIAN BUSINESS SCHOOLS IN THE 21ST CENTURY

Enrolment in cutting edge teaching has extended as of around 6.65 million out of 1995 to just about 12 million of each 2005. Example is on a incredibly basic level correspondent to for club preparing. The criticalness of Indian society schools lies added in the setting that 68 percent of the Indian citizens will be in the 22-multiyear age get together by 2020. This is the best increasingly open entrance for Indian youth while the world will look towards them with their picked up faculty in various fields. Furthermore, this illustration will be also support by the turning weak of the a load over the US, Europe, China, Canada and Japan, along these lines there will be a lack of power globally

As, an ever increasing number of youthful Indians are making progress toward a superior life, in these testing times, couple of significant inquiries emerge. Is the instruction framework prepared for this flood? It is safe to say that they are getting great quality training? Are there youthful qualified educators, libraries, gear and offices? Of the numerous Bschool rankings directed in the nation consistently, parameters focused are foundation physical, learning focuses, showing helps; instruction process-personnel, look into, consultancy, productions and Management Development Programs (MDPs); scholastic programmes– affirmation, educational modules, conveyance frameworks; social obligation; situation and industry border. Most affiliations are establish to set up unprecedented physical and educational structure yet not so in dissimilar components.

Moreover, the natural world of a base did not depend upon the part of structure alone, yet additionally on different much more in like manner key parts. The most exceedingly loathsome zone of execution among greater bit of the B-schools has be the deprived labor force and nonappearance of research preface (Sinha, .2007)

Most B-schools require to be grateful for that they are not in the matter of just dispersal data but quite in giving and creation knowledge. For this they have to put resources into showing signs of improvement personnel enhancing aptitudes of the current workforce, creating research focuses etc.(Baxi and Sahay, 2005). To be sure, even the greatest of the B-schools including IIMs, today enclose an absence of effort force. Furthermore near is an issue of cut off of staff with the large business. Quality and ability of employees are reflected in the preparation and course. Deficient is being complete in an area of investigate either since of the colossal preparing burdens administered on staff at the lower rung schools. Sound mix of both field fill in and furthermore study hall teaching is a certain necessity. There is a growing affirmation that workforce should direct research, raise resources for investigate and disseminate reliably in reputed journals (Dayal, 2002). These must choose their evaluation and rousing power portions. Qualified staff envision future needs better and make courses to meet them. Their investigation and conveyance attract industry and others to work with them on real issues.

One of the Ranking survey coordinated by IMRB International in 2007 driven by All India Management Association (AIMA) highlights the movements and upgrades lately. Of the endorsed B-schools, 199 partook in the overview. The review hurls rising patterns like more candidates, educational module changes, more prominent internationalization, upward development in pay rates, , better situation records , upgrades in innovation and framework. In the meantime, the discoveries draw out, the wide groupings which exist among the various classes of B-schools

Looking pushed planning in totality, an aggregate of 17,625 schools and 317 universities exist in India. Unexpectedly, till walk 2007, National Assessment and Accreditation Council (NAAC), a self-choice body set up by government in 1994 to ensure quality, could demand only 3, 942 schools and 140 universities in the country. Their examination relies on two or three parameters like purposes behind restriction of work control, straightforwardness of books, sports working conditions, structure, etc. This proposes around 75 % of schools and 56 % of universities have never been hated for quality measures by the body set up for the reason. Among the schools that have been avow by NAAC, only 245 colleges are in the A range, 1,785 in the B run and 668 in the C make and these could be kept an eye out for as high, medium and low quality schools, which breaker 9%, 66%, and 25% wholeheartedly of those that have been assessed

School Grants Commission(UGC) has around 14, 000 schools under its space, notwithstanding, in its own rise make assessments, just around 38% fulfill the base conditions required for requesting and budgetary assistance. In a diagram enveloped by UGC, quality measures of 111 universities and 1473 schools were checked which included parameters like utmost of teachers, understudy educator degrees, number of books open, and an enormous social gathering of fundamental workplaces like motels, sports, get together lounge area, guaranteed rooms, etc. The exposures for this condition likewise shows a negative picture–just 8% schools got An outline, 37% were given B consider and around 36% were named C consider. This is the condition when essentially some insignificant quantifiable parameters are being considered.

In the business school relationship, of the 1300 business universities in India, not using all methodology a single school happens to be among the authentic 50 in any far reaching rankings. Quality clearly is something where schools need to focus, to measure up with their mates in the western world. This comes as a huge test in the season of globalization, where exceptional business colleges need to move center from national redirection to general targets. To accomplish this, Indian school have started activities, for example, setting up worldwide linkages which incorporate, trade of workforce and understudies, advances joint research and counseling ventures. Be that as it may, progressing in the direction of official approval, both national and comprehensive will be a decisive and viable device in guarantee quality (Chandra, 2003).

4.2 QUALITY IN THE EDUCATION SECTOR

Quality in advanced teaching is more big than one would wait for, mostly on the grounds that, terms like quality, responsibility, and evaluation are utilized to some degree reciprocally (Ewell, 1991, 1993). Quality is a procedure or a way of reasoning whereby hierarchical members verifiably see their work as profitable, quantifiable, and ready to be moved forward. The asset see holds that the idea of a foundation of cutting edge training can be directed by assessing its internal resources: the amount of books in its library, the quantity of work force with terminal degrees, size of the enrichment, notoriety, and so forth. Be that as it may, inner images of value were not any more the most real proportions of fulfillment requested by an undeniably advanced education customer. "It has turned out to be clear that understudies, the essential clients of the establishment, need and need more than library books and an amazing arrangement of staff degrees counted toward the finish of the school index" (Seymour, 1992). These commerce universities gave significant aptitudes about the standards of exchange and trade to partners and executives from fields, for example, putting aside money, convey, and bookkeeping. After India's self-government in 1947, business preparation, which was connected with "babu-ism" and in this manner did not have a solid economic wellbeing, began to develop. While trying to upgrade professional abilities, the Lawmaking body of India showed big business as a third tributary of field at the assistant school level, discipline and verbalizations being the other two.

The undergrad trade universities additionally looked to offer abilities integral to general society bookkeeping calling, as clear in the idea of their center courses: business financial matters, bookkeeping, administration, managing an account hypothesis, inspecting, and cost bookkeeping, all underscoring hypothetical and connected comprehension of business exchanges. Be that as it may, even at this stage, business instruction (trade) was not implied, according to the general public, for the mentally and scholastically skilled understudies. Savvy understudies were relied upon t o join the discipline watercourse at the helper school level, and take organize stream at the train level in one of the Indian

Institutes of skill, colleges, or additional explicit establishment. They by after that joined affiliation as explicit supervisor, and climb the relationship unit.

A move in the monetary wealthy of commerce direction started happening amidst the 1980s. Two significant powers were affecting everything. Regardless, rivalry for school level getting ready injury up savage, as the puncture in the gauge of certifications at the head understudy program and the number long-term ahead commencing the chief schools delivered for the discipline stream. Second, as affiliation in progress to create they started employing business moves on from the schools at the lesser official level, frequently upheld by some in-organization official preparing program, as the head designing universities neglected to meet their developing requirements for official work force. Therefore, society started seeing business instruction as a reasonable elective international ID to enter the corporate world at the official, instead of the administrative, level. Numerous guardians urged their youngsters to take up the business stream at the auxiliary school level, with a view that their children could perform decently well in the exchange space and get a magnificent corporate position without living with the extraordinary forceful strain to surpass desires academically in the science streams. Likewise, the social cost of exchange related preparing was inside and out lower than the social cost of science-related instruction, in light of the fact that, not at all like the last mentioned, the previous did not require research facilities and other testing offices. Thusly, it was less demanding for the legislature and the instructive foundations to take care of the demand for trade training.

4.3 ADMINISTRATION FOCUSED BUSINESS EDUCATION IN INDIA

A basic development that was in series was the capacity that was life form made among trade and the friendship part of the commerce getting ready. The purpose of merger of Commerce direction was on organization a solid establishment concerning the learning of business connections and strategies, on the whole from the fiscal point and secretarial viewpoints. Strikingly, friendship planning intense on structure getting a number of answers about guideline language business and its dissimilar points of incarceration, given its assistant and the marketplace scene.. Along these lines, association planning was proposed for the graduated class and expert dimensions, concentrated on supporting future pioneers who might lead the hush-hush and open bit involvement with a conclusion of social charge

The Indian Institute of Social discipline, a code organization of higher education intense just on graduate class and doctoral endeavors, developed India's first friendship agenda in 1948, future to successfully plan work, make and spread the information required for coordinating mechanical undertakings in India. After a short time, in 1949, Catholic social request set up Xavier Labor Relations foundation (XLRI) at Jamshedpur – the capital of TISCO (Tata Group). The essential locales of exhorting included different leveled progress, experience plan, and cash related exercises.

Maintained by the postponed consequences of these early activities, the Government related for and selected up a yield beginning the Ford establishment in 1961 to dispatch two Indian Institutes of Management (IIM) - one at Calcutta (West Bengal), and the further at Ahmedabad (Gujarat). This give way depended on serving exchange American business preparation information plus models to different country, and necessary certified joint attempt with an American commerce college for enable the exchanging of learning. The IIM at Calcutta shaped joint effort by means of the Sloan School of organization at MIT for employees and representative technique group and the IIM at Ahmedabad set up relative investment by Harvard Business School. IIM at Calcutta adjusted the Sloan's occasion tactic and lab preparing, and searched for after an examination and planning thinking progressively spun around quantitative and operational bits of association. Then again, following HBS, IIM at Ahmedabad in progress the case technique for education in India, and drove persuading examination organized towards making cases on Indian affiliations and setting, with a supplement on dynamic key joining. The assignment of IIM's was to professionalize Indian friendship through instructing, explore, preparing, foundation fabricating and counseling. They likewise had an order to professionalize crucial segments of the economy, especially horticulture, training, wellbeing, transportation, populace control, vitality, and open organization. Towards this end, they helped dispatch a few specific administration training school.

Progression both in information and status occur in the midst of the 1990s. Innumerable relations entered India, and attempt to utilize business alumnae for their association getting prepared positions. Household organizations additionally stuck to this same pattern endeavoring to rival multinational companies. Organizations found that the aptitudes of business moves on from the trade stream fluctuated enormously crosswise over various universities, and missed the mark regarding the requests of the official positions in an aggressive world. Specifically, trade graduates had great bookkeeping aptitudes, however needed imperative promoting, social, and tasks abilities. They had frail establishing in oral and composed relational abilities, basic reasoning and basic perusing aptitudes, and in addition in data innovation and cooperation aptitudes that were winding up extremely applicable amid the 1990s. Therefore, given the expenses of preparing trade graduates, organizations offered colossal premium for those with a MBA degree. Seeing the exploit of MBA behavior, and deals from understudies and affiliations, school started looking prepare as a snappy sales and ongoing offering MBA programs. They could attain this by using their there exchange work ability to set up some commerce courses. Regardless, there are necessary costs of exhibit a MBA program, which uphold the progress of animatedly dexterous and adaptable BBA (Bachelor's in Business Administration) program at the substitute level.

Precisely when veered from the MBA program, the BBA assignments referenced less qualified workforce (for example staff with logically compelled work understanding and with doctoral farthest point) and offered more inmate understudy body (since single wolf's undertakings were dependably of three years, while the ace's activities propped up only two years). The BBA adventures offered a anthology of center, fix up to the requirements of the close to business, in spaces, for instance, publicizing, bargains affiliation, travel affiliation, remote trade, rural improvement, exchange transportation, neighborhood designing, stock connections, actuarial science, try and commerce mail.

The creation stability of the BBA training is presently making an emergency for the situating of the customary undergrad business degree programs. The understudies are progressively offering inclination to the BBA programs, than to the swap programs. Clearing up the action of the student swap certificate has transformed into an imperative test, in light of the way that huge academic resources are starting at now placed assets into the student business program.

In the intervening time, organization establishment continued create. With the assistance of leaning made by the initiate IIM's, two more IIMs were built up – in Bangalore (Karnataka) in 1973, and in Lucknow (Uttar Pradesh). In late 1990s, two extra IIMs, one at Calicut (Kerala) and the additional at Indore (Madhya Pradesh) be put up to moreover decentralize and create organization capital and capacity each through Indium. The idea of business program in the scholar enrolment has shaped from under 15% out of 1970 to over 22% by 2000.

4.4 NATURE OF BUSINESS EDUCATION IN INDIA

There is an incredible assorted variety of business training in India and it may not be significant to think about a wide range of schools in an examination of value. As of not long ago, the best business colleges have worked as good examples for the rest; anyway various business colleges are endeavoring to make their very own territorial or sectoral advancement specialties. These quality activities have been mostly upheld by an acknowledgment at the national approach level of a need to adjust an asset distribution technique concentrated on 'making islands of radiance in a mass of middling class with a procedure that guides "little improvement in extensive figure of brass tacks" (Natarajan, 2003). A more wide plan concern recognize with the clear Catch 22 in the middle of Excellence and Equity. To distinguish the best educational basis, one wants to think about a few criteria. No organization may have an outright favorable position in all things; in this manner it is essential to support the improvement of similar preferred standpoint of every business college by perceiving the estimation of their self-defining, enterprising activities.

Despite the fact that there are numerous issues in making examinations crosswise over business colleges, there are some all-inclusive measuring sticks for estimating worth in commerce tuition, and we will utilize the normal ones: Nature of understudies jointly with the declaration procedure, (2) Pedagogy, (3) Placement (4) Faculty advancement and (5) Infrastructure.

Nature of students:

The nature of understudies toward the inside business college is critical to believe. As depicted before, customarily, instruction in business was not seen as the instructive way of the most splendid understudies. In any case, as of now, getting acknowledged into an all-around viewed business college is viewed as exceptionally alluring vocation.

Dependably around 100,000 beyond any doubt contender take Common admittance Test or the corroboration primer of the IIMs. Of these 1,100 will be chosen to oblige one of the IIM's. For example, IIM Ahmedabad has 200 seats. Everything measured request model are high. Everything careful, the IIMs have been seen as the world's figure 1 to the degree their selectivity, and trouble of receiving recruitment into (Times of India, Feb 19, 2003).

A fascinating piece of the corroboration system is the practice of different solicitation tests and events by different business university, not the smallest amount bit like the US where GMAT is used as a normal test score. The administration of India tried to exhibit a normal guarantee test for the b-schools in spite of the Supreme Court of India expelled that endeavor. The Court chosen that "private instructive foundations have their very own identity, and keeping in mind the end goal to keep up their environment and conventions, it is essential that they have the privilege to pick and select the understudies who can be conceded." (Goswami, 2003). The compensation of a standard way test are mention to be invalidated and group will feel there is a need to expand a few degrees of equivalencies in the middle of scores of different official approval tests, so the probability of the in order sources can be separated as of the likelihood of the informative system while creation relationship amid different b-schools. An palpable bit of b-schools in India is the broadly appealing mixture of understudy profile. Since affiliation prepare is most important at the graduate class level, certain contenders start from a blend of scholastic stream, for example, designing, human sciences, science, business, and prescription, in this manner giving an extremely rich between disciplinary classroom encounter. Be that as it may, the majority of the MBA understudies in India are generally bursting, and they enter the graduate class program as the crow flies after their understudy heading. Despite the way that unyielding the Indian establishment give some added weight for work understanding, a more remarkable bit of understudies are with no work affiliation. This is in the vicinity of in both the best engineered and second estimation schools. This is rather than the US, where standard graduated class understudies have something like 3-4 years of work fusion .Recently, before long, Harvard Business School has ongoing suffering contender without work understanding; it in the end reviews contenders on scholastic capacity, individual qualities, and authority encounter; where casual or formal administration encounter outside work setting is likewise perceived. The compensation of relating business hypothesis to their own work familiarity may consequently not happen, but relatively there is required to be more stranded receptiveness to stumble on out about elective plans of action.

Teaching method

Scholastic quality isn't really dependent upon the understudy quality. More savvy understudies and better asset enrichments positively encourage the showing procedure, and may likewise create a more successful learning process. Be that as it may, scholarly quality might be upgraded by obtaining better quality understudies as well as by enhancing the nature of understudies. The vital inquiry is what abilities work together understudies require? Lately, US business colleges have been scrutinized for not teaching understudies in aptitudes important to business. In a normally cited report on or after Booz, Allen and Hamilton, selling instruction has vanished under response for not prepare understudies to speak to the issues of business (Doria et al., 2003). The creator put it to somebody more "courses in correspondence, authority, HR, brain research, and different fields that furnish graduates with aptitudes indispensable to adequately overseeing individuals and group driven associations". They propose that business colleges ought to require no less than two of each 10 go course to base on such subjects. In their assessment of the best 10 trade colleges, they saw that basically half require no under two workshops on person or conclusive relationship.

The condition in India look positive. Inside lessons obtainable in XLRI are given in Appendix 2. As strength be watched, present are various lessons in the relationship of persons. For example, XLRI requires three lessons in Organizational performance. There is along these lines impressive consideration paid to abilities that outcome in administrative achievement.

A critical component basic to most selling college in India is the compulsory summer familiarity that understudies could do with to try among their first and moment years. Understudies are relied on to exertion with business liaison for two months at any rate. This takes subsequent to area level position in the US, neighboring to all understudies are required to knowledge this. This engages school to demonstrate area setting in their educational everyday jobs, going past basically utilizing the American examining material and talking about Japanese standards for the all-purpose substance. Further, a enormous bunch of these schools have strive to consider the fastidious needs of the next-door liaison by offering explicit in turn based sectoral program, for example, by plus genuine undertakings and producing solid interfaces with the business.

Significant assorted variety exists in the school methodology. The case-based and experimental methodology isn't all around utilized. In customary business colleges, educational programs are impacted by the conventional syllabi-arranged scholarly instructional method. The staff hurry through points with a view to terminate the course, and convey address utilize the textile given. There is on a regular basis just a constrained stress on the advancement of basic and explanatory philosophy and a feeling of logical request, perception, issue conclusion, and critical thinking. Thus, these graduates indicate lacking specialized and social abilities; and exhibit a hypothetical and self-situated state of mind. Numerous organizations have been worried that graduates do not have a feeling of social nationality and administration. Most organization needed to put "re-training" program set up, to reorient the alumnae to the business they were enlist to. Guided by the state of mind in business agreed projects, it was generally acknowledged that eminence may be improved by harder examination, where they are solicit to get ready with huge amount from subjects. Notwithstanding, as a general rule, evaluators ordinarily bring down their desire and honor stamps generously with the goal that the extent of understudies scoring distinctive evaluations pretty much stays consistent. As of late, there is an expanded spotlight on endeavoring to likewise test on basic application skills, for example, one including venture work. Examinations remain a critical component of the educational programs, guided by a rationality that each advantageous action must be checked on, observed, evaluated, and sustained back to expand productivity and adequacy (Natarajan, 2003).

4.5 DIFFICULTIES IN BUSINESS EDUCATION

The most key test for big business course in India pivot how the soothing preparing is compelled to the best estimation schools. The degree of understudies proceeding ahead from these schools is miniscule showed up contrastingly in association with necessities of the country. The course that there is such a multifaceted nature between the best estimation and next estimation prompts different issues that we will investigate underneath. It must, in any case, be seen that the second section of business university, more than ever the ones that have through over the degree of the most modern two decades, cover other than made two or three pockets of worth, which are of soaring bore. In our test of the likelihood of commerce affiliations, we raise that the best estimation commerce establishment have legitimize based determination. Be that as it may, to do well in the choice, an understudy ought to have had top class earlier training. By and large, such training is costly and not moderate by the dominant part. So the playing field isn't even in any case. Further, the passageway tests are in English, which cripples a generally splendid understudy who examined in country territories and is less acquainted with English. Subsequently, in spite of the legitimacy based placement test, as a general rule, getting induction into the IIM's isn't absurd that is inside the array of in general Indians.

On the off chance that without a doubt the nature of training in most different organizations misses the mark regarding that at top level school, for example, IIM's (as the best in start wages earn by IIM alumnae propose), at that point one can't expect moves on from top level schools to enhance their work environment as they could if their companion gather likewise got an improved nature of administration instruction. Another issue with the enormous distinction in nature of instruction prompts an elitist mindset. As organizations achieve achievement, some wind up wrapped up in their notoriety, and lose center around genuine achievements. This demeanor rubs off to understudies moving on from such organizations. Frequently, candidates who gain bringing on into any of the best train tend to see themselves in exclusive terms, and institute conduct, for example, looking behind at those from jiffy level schools. Be that as it may, considering that the greater part of their partners in their work environment will have degrees from less renowned establishments, such a state of mind will come in the method for collaboration that is ending up progressively imperative in associations today. An attention on genuine achievements as opposed to taking shelter in having a place with a world class aggregate is probably going to make these graduates more powerful.

Despite the fact that there are numerous explanations behind this wide distinction in nature of industry training in India, one indispensable reason is in all probability going to be the absence of a body that all establishments admire set benchmarks – like the AACSB in USA. Despite the fact that there is a zenith body – the All India gathering for Technical lessons (AICTE) that is in charge of characterizing the fundamental system for nature of the business-training and affirming passage and development of all institutions1 , there are by and by, numerous issues that dent its adequacy.

AICTE requires amazing like 1,200 contact hours for the MBA plan, notwithstanding two months of summer impermanent job and pasture ventures, partitioned more than 2 years for the around the clock pattern, and 3 years for the low persistence and partition learning group. The candidate are to be accepted based on a local or defensive level poised assessment to survey their condition and aversion for learning of organization, completion in gather dialog plus talk with, social and individuality quality tests for capable aptitude, and earlier erudite record and work sympathetic. An collection of educational methodologies are supported past addresses, including contextual investigations, gathering and individual activities, class assignments, venture work and introductions, pretend, and administration diversions. Each center workforce is required to instruct up to six course per year, with an additional four course stack similar time committed to examine, official expansion programs, scholastic union, and counseling. Prescribed workforce understudy proportion is 1:60. Every basis is required to have at least 7 middle full-time labor force, who at that point fill in as grapples for the low maintenance, visiting or visitor staff proportionate to no less than three extra full time personnel. A library with somewhere around 30 diaries, and something like 200 titles in every one of the branches of knowledge, should likewise be kept up. At last, adequate PC and instructional development and helps are necessary. These criterion typify the base passage hindrances. As of late, to energize a procedure of nonstop audit, AICTE has additionally propelled National Board of Accreditation (NBA), utilizing a benchmarking framework concerning variables, for example, physical foundation, nature of data sources, and personnel preparing. Nonetheless, falling measures of schools avowed by AICTE drop its validity. It is accounted for that numerous selling colleges got AICTE backing based on appealing undertaking designs, which never got actualized, so some of them worked "for all intents and purposes from sheds and carports." (Raghunath, 1998)

The finish is that most bschools contain on oath off look for official recognition under NBA. A additional factor restrict the importance of what may have credibly been a national official credit standard is the expediency of substitutes. For example, in 1998, All India administration Association (AIMA) utilize ISO 9000 to build up a quality avowal structure, known as QBS 1000. QBS 1000 set of courses determined and evaluated b-school's worth and form and ensure their talent crosswise over critical and enthralling parameters. The QBS 1000 framework was future to assess quality at 100 or more organization related with AIMA (Raghunath, 1998). Numerous additional free b-schools the same discovered ISO an alluring option for creating and mark their establishments. In any case, now, it isn't evident that there is any broadly utilized accreditation framework.

Regardless of the absence of consistency in nature of business instruction, popularity for dealing graduates and development have prompted the two inspired patterns – the growth of private commerce colleges and meadow players and the long-drawn-out globalization of business preparation.

CHAPTER 5
Accountability and Transparency in PPB Systems

As an interest in individuals and as a device of financial strategy has provided a foundation for flow endeavors to extend and make more particular anticipating instructive improvement (PED). Estimations of labor necessities from one viewpoint, and of social interest for instruction on the other, have set the phase for extra addressing of the outcomes from training, for more evaluation, and for comprehension of the value of more prominent accuracy in arranging.

This examination is composed, basically, as a guide in stepping toward more point by point instructive planning» The investigation is isolated into five areas. The primary manages what is an arranging, programming, planning (PPB) framework. The second area identifies with why getting ready for instructive advancement inside a PPB framework. In the accompanying three segments, every one of the significant segments that include a PPB framework is examined,, For instance, segment three manages the basic parts of making arrangements for instructive advancement, the characterizing of goals , and the organizing of exercises for the showcase of store distributions among purposes. Area four shows a synopsis of the substance ""of program examination and a representation of a methodology toward investigation. In the last area the reason and procedures of a multi-year program and money related arrangement are exhibited.

PPB framework

PPB frameworks have come to be characterized in to some degree distinctive routes as the essential ideas have been adjusted by legislatures of fluctuating sizes, complexities of obligations, and worries of staff work force and officialdom* We characterize PPB here to mean an arrangement of request about, and administration of, open projects and exercises by goals. It is basically a strategy for legislative programming, by targets.

The detailing and appraisal of those goals, examination of elective projects that can accomplish them, estimation of asset prerequisites, - and responsibility for program results are central to the framework o We see PPB with regards to a framework - a framework for uniting educational archives that as a normal procedure of administration can furnish approach authorities with progressively and better data.

The data that would be given incorporates precisely analyzed purposes, program expenses, and potential program brings about accomplishing indicated purposes through different program alternatives, both promptly and in the more drawn out run. The everyday practice of the framework requires explanatory documentation preceding authority spending plan and program suggestions. What's more, as a framework, PPB requires, the systematic handling of diagnostic work with the goal that the planning is suitable for the cycle of work in spending plan préparât!on. It is a framework for:

(I) Helping to accomplish government by goals;

(ii) Formulating programs in connection to operationally characterized objectives]

(iii) Generating new program plans and particulars;

(iv) Assembling all out program costs; and

(v) Analyzing those projects as per indicated criteria for estimation.

Critically, PPB is a framework that gives an event to social development and advancement. By requiring a look for choices, the framework opens the way to age of choices and thought of different choices; at' minimum it guarantees a more incite and more noteworthy acknowledgment of appraisal of new thoughts. It gives an event; as well, for the thought of interfacing and between related exercises that fill normal needs (both in people in general and private circles). That is, it sets the phase for between office discourse and correspondence in requiring an arrangement of aggregate expenses and generally speaking system adequacy.

For instance, numerous administration divisions are worried about instructive accomplishment; training can't be considered as an intrigue selective tc the offices or services of instruction. Components of the PPB procedure by and large are not new, but rather their blend and methodical application to instruction and other open issues is. As showed, before, these components have come to be portrayed in different ways, yet we characterize them as far as

(I) Structural perspectives;

(ii) Analytical perspectives; and

(iii) The correlative criticism, or responsibility, angles.

In the work on these components,, a progression of archives has been defined] these reports are the apparatuses through which the PPB framework is actualized. Notwithstanding assessment thinks about, they are:

(a) The program structure and articulation of destinations;

(b) Program investigations (cost-adequacy examinations) and memorandai and

(c) The multi-year program and budgetary arrangement.

The parts of the PPB framework, the narrative devices, and the procedures are delineated in Table 1,, Preparation of the few reports of a PPB framework requires-

(I) Clarifying and determining a definitive objectives or targets of every movement for which an administration spending plans cash;

(ii) Gathering contributing exercises Into far reaching classifications or projects to accomplish the predetermined goals;;

(iii) Examining as a nonstop procedure how well every movement or program has done - Its viability - as a first1 venture toward enhancing or notwithstanding killing it;

(iv) dissecting proposed changes or new program; recommendations: to perceive how successful they might be in accomplishing program objectives;

(v) Projecting the whole expenses of every proposition not: just for; the main year but rather for a few resulting years

(vi) Formulating an arrangement, situated to some degree on the examination of program cost and adequacy, that prompts execution through the financial plan.

5.1 PROGRAM OBJECTIVES

The announcements of goals of governments, and of training as¡a capacity of governments, are crucial to program organizing, program investigation, longer range program arranging, and program, assessment. Except if it is clear what yields are being looked for, there is basically no chance to get of knowing whether offices are accomplishing them by the projects embraced and consumptions made.

Table 1: parts, apparatuses and procedures of arranging, programming, planning

Component Elements	Documentary Tools	Processes Required
Structural	Statement of objectives	- Formulating and defining objectives - Formulating criteria of measurement
	Programme structure	- Classifying programmes and activities into a hierarchy - Assigning expenditures to classification of programme categories and elements
	Multi-year programme and financial plan	- Summarizing decisions taken in output and cost terms - Projecting programme levels ahead - Projecting workload costs of current programme ahead
Analytical	Programme analysis study (Problem definition statement)	- Defining objectives - Defining criteria of measurement - Formulating programme options
	(Cost-effectiveness studies)	- Developing model for analysis - Collecting data relevant to criteria of effectiveness - Collecting relevant cost data - Carrying out data analysis
Evaluative	Programme evaluation studies	- Collecting data on programme performance - Designing experiments where indicated

Plan and meaning of purposes necessitate that bureau officers and office heads get some information about their objectives openly benefit » What is it that is being looked for by method for results or items? Or on the other hand, what needs doing and for whom? Detailing likewise propels an investigation into the accompanying zones; Why is every action as of now performed being performed?

For instance, what are the motivations behind 'HR programmes5? Is the principle goal to raise the level of yield in the country - to expand, that is, the nation*s efficiency and: gross national item? Or then again, is the goal to enhance the level of living and per capita pay of the poorest in the country? Or then again, is the main role to build up the scholarly limit of the country for social interests?

These reasons vary, thus. essentially would the criteria by which advancement could be judged,, The kind of program that is outlined would likewise vary., contingent on the decision of reason made o If every one of these intentions are looked for, each still should be recognized independently and advancement toward each outcome estimated independently« Those who must choose can make a decision in what blend they would stress national financial development, remedy of the most exceedingly bad pockets of neediness (regardless of whether the national yield is brought up in result), and national social development«

5.2 PROGRAM STRUCTURES

The program structure itself shows a chain of importance of program exercises c At the highest levels are the general classifications that mirror the projects intended to accomplish the major goals of the administration o The second and lower levels show continuously smaller groupings serving more restricted destinations.

As the classifications progress toward becoming smaller in scope at the lower levels, it is conceivable to order inside one sub-classification correlative, and furthermore substitute, program ways to deal with the accomplishment of crucial targets,, The most minimal levels of any structure would be made out of exercises and projects that are expected as particular means for pushing toward the bigger destinations.

The presentation of projects in connection to goals gives data on programs diverse in some courses from that contained in spending records currently submitted to governing bodies. As a rule, spending archives are 'line' thing spending plans as opposed to program-arranged spending plans; full program costs don't generally show up in a similar spending classification.

Usage of a PPB framework does not necessitate that the spending design be modified., but rather it requires that for programming purposes uses be gathered as far as program targets instead of as far as the things purchased, In a few locales spending groups have been altered«

The order chain of command of classes, sub-classifications, et cetera is fundamentally a conditional gathering to be enhanced and modified as required by changing issues and issue emphasis» Basically the program structure is a data record to be utilized by strategy authorities as an estimated guide or show of the decisions that have been made among projects and exercises. A variety of consumptions as per a program structure may tend to appear, for instance, the amount of the country's aggregate planned assets is given to HR. Inside the HR cate» shocking it may indicate what amount is given to social insurance and the amount to scholarly improvement of the populace. At a lower level the arrangement gathering may be intended to elucidate for strategy authorities how the financial plan for instruction identifies with the financial plan for work preparing and work position and from among the activity preparing and situation programs, the relative sums for at work preparing as appeared differently in relation to more formal specialized preparing.

5.3 PROGRAM ANALYSIS

Integral to the PPB exertion is examination of projects to evaluate the underlying detail of goals,, to break down the likely yields in program results as far as the destinations as surveyed from different program choices, and to gauge add up to expenses of the few alternatives applicable to the program choice. Arranging, programming, planning frameworks, as frameworks, are best connected on an administration wide premise in which characterized goals apply to the whole scope of legislative activity» (all inclusive is being characterized here to mean an autonomous burdening spending choice unit.)

The administration wide exertion is an endeavor to increase better comprehension of the scope of projects and of offices worried about the samé or comparative goals. It endeavors to give a procedure inside which offices or services of instruction, for instance, may. See the extent of current administrations under their bearing that is essential to fulfilling the objectives of different divisions or of the legislature all in all correspondingly, branches of training inside this procedure may better fathom the commitment that non-instructive offices make to the mission of scholarly improvement of a populace. At the point when financial advancement is a focal government reason, the exhaustiveness of ways to deal with organizing the PPB framework's work and investigation winds up basic.

Comprehensiveness in objective setting and organizing makes program investigation the beginning stage of the PPB procedure for branches of educationj particularly in the creating countries. The examination procedure is a binding together and looking at one» On the one hand,, outcomes are surveyed as far as costs,, both those that are prompt and those that are certain for ensuing periods because of quick activity.

Then again, they are surveyed regarding advantages or program adequacy. Demonstrating expenses and viability next to each other for different program choices gives new data that can settle on judicious choices more probable. Examination basically includes a decrease of complex issues into their part sections with the goal that each fragment can be contemplated. Inquiries of certainty can be subjected through this procedure to the trial of watched involvement.

Those parts of the issue that include esteem judgment can be independently recognized and the premise of the judgment, made express. From one viewpoint, a cost-adequacy examination may utilize, if appropriate, huge numbers of the strategies of arithmetic, activities investigate, financial matters, and so forth.

On the other, cost-adequacy examination may require not any more specialized advancement than the pulling together of effectively existing information in an important and enlightening way. Investigations may likewise draw upon different specialized and non-specialized examinations already done. Proposals made based on examination inside the methods of a PPB framework are introduced in approach papers named 'program memoranda'.

The 'program reminder' is a record covering one noteworthy program zone or a noteworthy part of a noteworthy program territory. Its motivation is to show real program strategy discoveries particular suggestions, and the explanations behind these proposals, including a rundown of the investigations that have been made. It is submitted preceding point by point spending planning

CONCLUSION

A business creates in course of time with complexities. With expanding complexities dealing with the business has turned into a troublesome errand. The need of presence of administration has expanded massively. Administration is fundamental for business worries as well as for banks, schools, universities, doctor's facilities, inns, religious bodies, magnanimous trusts and so forth. Each specialty unit has its very own few goals. These goals can be accomplished with the organized endeavors of a few work force. Crafted by various people are legitimately co-ordinated to accomplish the goals through the procedure of administration doesn't involve squeezing a catch, pulling a lever, issuing orders, examining benefit and misfortune proclamations, declaring guidelines and controls. Or maybe it is the ability to figure out what will happen to the identities and satisfaction of whole individuals, the ability to shape the fate of a country and of the considerable number of countries which make up the world." Peter F. Drucker has expressed in his well-known book "The Practice of Management" that, "the rise of administration as a basic, a particular and driving social organization is a significant occasion in social history. Seldom in mankind's history has another establishment demonstrated crucial so rapidly and even less regularly as another foundation landed with so little restriction, so little aggravation thus little discussion?" Management is an indispensable part of the monetary existence of man, which is a composed gathering movement. It is considered as the crucial establishment in the cutting edge social association set apart by logical idea and mechanical developments. Either type of administration is basic wherever human endeavors are to be attempted all in all to fulfill needs through some profitable movement, occupation or calling.

It is administration that manages man's gainful exercises through facilitated utilization of material assets. Without the administration given by administration, the assets of creation remain assets and never progress toward becoming generation.

Administration is the incorporating power in all sorted out action. At whatever point at least two individuals cooperate to accomplish a typical goal, they need to facilitate their exercises; they likewise need to sort out and use their assets so as to improve the outcomes. Not just in business undertakings where expenses and incomes can be found out precisely and equitably yet additionally in benefit associations, for example, government, healing facilities, schools, clubs, and so on., rare assets including men, machines, materials and cash must be coordinated in a gainful relationship, and used effectively towards the accomplishment of their ladies.

Therefore, administration isn't extraordinary to business associations yet regular to a wide range of social associations. Administration has accomplished an advantageous significance as of late. We are on the whole personally connected with numerous sorts of associations, the most ubiquitous being the legislature, the school and the healing facility. Indeed, more of significant social errands are being sorted out on a foundation premise.

Medicinal consideration, training, amusement, water system, lighting, sanitation, and so on which commonly used to be the worry of the individual or the family, are currently the space of substantial associations, in spite of the fact that, associations other than business don't talk about administration, they all need administration. It is the particular organ of a wide range of associations since they all need to use their restricted assets most proficiently and viably for the accomplishment of their objectives. It is the most crucial powers in the fruitful execution of a wide range of sorted out social exercises.

Significance of administration for the improvement of immature economies has been perceived amid the last one and a half decade. There is a critical hole between the administration adequacy in created and immature nations. It is appropriately held that advancement is the capacity of capital, physical and material assets, as well as of their ideal use. Successful administration can deliver not just more yields of products and ventures with given assets, yet in addition extend them through better utilization of science and innovation. A higher rate of monetary development can be achieved in our nation through more proficient and powerful administration of our business and other social associations, even with existing physical and budgetary assets. That is the reason it is currently being progressively perceived that immature nations are in reality to some degree insufficiently oversaw nations. The rise of administration in present day times might be viewed as a critical improvement as the headway of current innovation. It has made conceivable association of financial movement in monster associations like the Steel Authority of India and the Life Insurance Corporation of India. It is to a great extent through the accomplishments of current administration that western nations have achieved the phase of mass utilization social orders, and it is to a great extent through more powerful administration of our financial and social foundations that we can enhance the personal satisfaction of our kin. It is the accomplishments of business administration that hold the expectation for the enormous masses in the underdeveloped nations that they can expel destitution and accomplish for themselves average ways of life.

Printed in the USA
CPSIA information can be obtained
at www.ICGtesting.com
CBHW020812260624
10675CB00002B/273